STUDIES IN THE UK ECONOMY

KT-452-127

Equity and efficiency

Margaret Wilkinson
University of Bradford

Series Editor
Bryan Hurl
Head of Economics, Harrow School

HEINEMANN
EDUCATIONAL

Heinemann Educational,
a division of Heinemann Publishers (Oxford) Ltd.
Halley Court, Jordan Hill, Oxford OX2 8EJ

OXFORD   LONDON   EDINBURGH
MADRID   ATHENS   BOLOGNA   PARIS
MELBOURNE   SYDNEY   AUCKLAND   SINGAPORE   TOKYO
IBADAN   NAIROBI   HARARE   GABORONE
PORTSMOUTH NH (USA)

First published 1993

93 94 95 96 97 10 9 8 7 6 5 4 3 2 1

British Library Cataloguing in Publication Data

A catalogue record for this book is available from the British Library

ISBN 0 435 33017 9

Typeset and illustrated by Taurus Graphics, Kidlington, Oxon.

Printed and bound in Great Britain by Clay Ltd, St Ives plc.

Acknowledgements

The Publishers would like to thank the following for permission to reproduce copyright material:
Andrew Cook for the article on p. 36–7; The Associated Examining Board for the questions on pp. 9, 20, 34, 76 and 89; Banx for the cartoons on pp. 7, 38 and 41; Central Statistical Office for the table on p. 80; The Commission of the European Communities for the extract on p. 43; Conservative Political Centre for the extract on p. 90; The *Economist* for the articles on pp. 37, 52 and 56; Fabian Society for ABC of Thatcherism, ed. G Wright on p. 90; The *Financial Times* for the articles on pp. 18, 36–7, 79 and 84; Frank Hahn for the article on p. 4; The *Guardian* for the extract on p. 65 and the cartoon by Austin on p. 12; The *Independent* for the cartoon by Geoff Thompson on p. 45; Institute of Economic Affairs for the extract on p. 51; Professor Layard for the extract on p. 84; Northern Examinations and Assessment Board for the questions on pp. 9, 20, 34, 42, 53 and 63; Oxford and Cambridge Schools Examination Board for the questions on pp. 20, 34, 42, 53, 63, 77 and 89; Penguin for the article on p. 8; Royal Bank of Scotland for the extract on p. 50; The *Times* for the extract on p. 35; University of Cambridge Local Examinations Syndicate for the questions on pp. 42, 53 and 64; University of London Examinations & Assessment Council for the questions on pp. 9, 20, 35, 53–4, 64, 76 and 77; University of Oxford Delegacy of Local Examinations for the question on p. 34; Welsh Joint Education Committee for the questions on pp. 10, 22 and 42.

The publishers have made every effort to contact the correct copyright holders. However, if any material has been incorrectly acknowledged, the Publishers will be pleased to make the necessary arrangements at the earliest opportunity.

Contents

Preface

It was observed by Richard Lipsey and Colin Harbury:

'Efficiency and equity are the two major goals of economic policy'.

Yet this is not quite how the standard texts treat these concepts. Generally, much is implicit rather than explicit.

Simply peruse the Introduction of this short book and you will realise that the author covers these topics in a very convincing and interesting way. You are recommended to use this book in conjunction with the new, rewritten, companion volume in the series, *Supply Side Economics*. Equity and efficiency now get the A-level treatment they require and deserve.

Bryan Hurl
Series Editor

Introduction

There are two principal criteria by which economic outcomes are judged: equity and efficiency. Efficiency is achieved if the output from an economy's resources is at a maximum *and* if this output is that which yields the greatest satisfaction, or utility, to consumers. In Chapter 1, which starts with a definition of welfare economics, there is a precise definition of efficiency which includes a discussion of the concept of Pareto efficiency. Chapter 1 also discusses equity, which is more difficult to define. It requires that there should be a fair distribution of welfare – that is, a fair distribution of the economy's goods and services. But there is no objective measure of fairness. For one person it is fair that those who put in the effort get the rewards, with only subsistence incomes for the rest. Another person would judge this to be most unfair.

Chapters 2 to 8 apply the ideas of equity and efficiency to a variety of economic issues. We find that frequently there is conflict between the two principles. For example, taxing workers' incomes to pay unemployment benefits may reduce the incentive to work. However, such conflict is not always the case: regulating monopoly or taxing polluters can be both efficient and fair.

Chapter 2 is about economic systems. The market system is efficient but inequitable; planning is inefficient but has the potential to be fair. However, the inefficiencies of the command economy appear to overwhelm any equity advantages and recently many planned economies have been rejected by their citizens, and an urgent task is to help them to develop market systems.

Chapters 3 and 4 compare competition and monopoly. Chapter 3 focuses on theory and Chapter 4 on policy. In Chapter 3 we discover that competition is efficient, and that monopoly is both inefficient (there is under-production) and unfair (consumers are exploited). However, the inefficiency argument is based on fairly restrictive assumptions, whereas in the real world monopoly may lead to lower costs, to innovation and to economic growth. If this happens, consumers benefit. Chapter 4 shows that British competition policy starts from the premise that the issue of monopoly is not clear-cut and that each case must be judged on its merits. The costs of monopoly are balanced against its potential benefits in terms of economies of scale, research and development, long-run growth and strength in

1

international markets. In the UK the aim is to *regulate* monopoly. This contrasts with the US approach which starts with the assumption that monopoly power is always bad and should be broken up.

Chapter 5 is about external costs, for example pollution and the greenhouse effect. External costs are both unfair, because they are imposed on third parties, and inefficient, because they reduce total welfare. There is no policy conflict between equity and efficiency. Chapter 6 defines and gives examples of external benefits. Goods which confer these benefits are produced in less than efficient quantities by the market, and we discover why this happens. The benefits of some goods are *all* external: these are public goods. Other goods provide both internal (private) and external benefits and so are known as mixed goods. Chapter 6 discusses both public and mixed goods, and the role the government plays in providing them.

Chapter 7 is about taxes. Taxes are judged by how efficient, or neutral, and how fair they are. Taxes distort choices, and a tax system is judged as efficient when it causes the minimum of such distortions. Taxes also change the distribution of income. A tax may take proportionately more from the rich and less from the poor (a progressive tax); or proportionately less from the rich and more from the poor (a regressive tax). We look at how the idea of equity can be applied to judging taxes, then British taxes and recent tax changes are assessed in terms of efficiency and equity.

Chapter 8 discusses poverty and redistribution. In the relief of poverty, equity and efficiency frequently conflict: what is fair is usually distortionary and so inefficient. Redistribution can be undertaken by fiscal methods (taxes and transfers), or by intervention in markets (minimum wages, rent controls and so on). Economists find that interference in markets is very inefficient and prefer fiscal means to alleviate poverty, though these too are non-neutral. They cause disincentives for taxpayers and the poverty trap for the low paid.

Chapter One

Welfare economics

'And the moral of that is – "The more there is of mine the less there is of yours".' 'Oh, I know', exclaimed Alice, who had not attended to this last remark. Lewis Carroll

Scarcity and choice

In all economies, people's wants for goods and services are unlimited but the resources to satisfy them are scarce. Choices must therefore be made about what goods and services to produce, how to produce them, and who should get them. Any economic system must undertake two functions, **allocation** and **distribution**:

- Resources must be allocated to the production of goods and services – to answer the *what?* and *how?* questions.
- Output must be distributed among consumers – there must be a solution to the *for whom?* question.

It is a goal of economic policy that allocation should be efficient and distribution should be equitable.

- **Efficiency** is concerned with resource allocation. It is achieved by maximizing consumers' economic welfare within a given income distribution.
- **Equity** is about how income should be distributed, and is more difficult to define as there is no consensus on what is a fair outcome – '. . . equity, like beauty, is in the mind of the beholder' (McLachan and Maynard), or ' "Fairness", like "needs", is in the eye of the beholder' (Friedman).

Welfare economics

The purpose of **welfare economics** is to assess how well the economy works when judged by the criteria of both efficiency and equity. It provides us with an economic theory of **social welfare**. It includes both description and prescription. It *describes* an efficient allocation of resources – the conditions necessary to achieve maximum welfare, given the distribution pattern. It also *prescribes* – it is **normative,** in particular on distribution.

Efficiency

There are different ways of defining efficiency. An engineer thinks of efficiency as maximizing output from given inputs. This amounts to the production of goods and services at minimum cost in terms of resources, which is productive or **technical efficiency.** An economist defines efficiency to include demand, so that it becomes maximizing the output of goods and services *which consumers demand* at minimum resource cost. This wider concept is known as economic or **allocative efficiency.**

Allocative efficiency is also known as **Pareto efficiency.** Vilfredo Pareto (1848–1923) argued that the allocation of resources was at a social 'optimum' if it was not possible to improve one consumer's welfare without making another worse off. Efficient allocation was attained if consumer A could not be made better-off without reducing B's welfare. (Given that diagrams are two-dimensional, we assume two consumers, and two goods in Fig. overleaf.) The Pareto criterion assumes that the distribution of income is given and it has nothing to say about equity. B may be very rich and A may be very poor, but if A's welfare cannot be improved except by reducing B's then the outcome is Pareto-efficient. (This should make it clear why Hahn objects to the use of the expression **'Pareto optimum'** – see the box.) There are many Pareto-efficient allocations and each one of them represents a different distribution of welfare.

. . . there are many Pareto-efficient allocations and each one of them will have a different distribution of welfare. Mrs Thatcher's [1] choice of a Pareto-efficient allocation, for instance, seems unlikely to correspond to any acceptable notion of distributive justice. Mr Benn's [2] choice on the other hand may not even be Pareto-efficient. In any case, the sloppy habit in the literature in speaking of a Pareto-optimum has misled many people into believing that their duty of serious moral argument has been fulfilled when they can show that some policy outcome is Pareto-efficient. As a matter of fact this is just the beginning of such an argument.

[1]Conservative Prime Minister 1979–90;   [2]Labour MP

Frank Hahn, 'Reflections on the invisible hand', *Lloyds Bank Review*, 1982

To attain Pareto efficiency there must be maximum output from given inputs, and maximum consumer utility from that output. Maximum output from given inputs means that productive efficiency, production of output at minimum opportunity cost, is part of allocative efficiency.

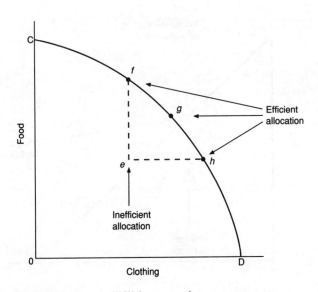

Figure 1 Production possibilities: maximum output

Productive efficiency can be illustrated using a **production possibility curve** (see Figure 1).

The line CD represents the maximum potential production of food and clothing. It shows that in order to have more clothing it is necessary to sacrifice some food production. It thus shows the *opportunity cost* of food in terms of clothing (and vice versa). Any point, any combination of food and clothing, on the production possibility curve CD is efficient. The quantity of each good is produced at minimum opportunity cost. Any point inside it is inefficient because production from the resources available could be increased (as far as the line CD). With given resources and technology, all points beyond CD are unattainable. Thus e is inefficient because it is possible to have more of both goods (g) or more of one good without any less of the other (f or h). At e it is possible, by increasing output, to make either or both consumers better-off without reducing the other's welfare.

Pareto efficiency also requires maximum consumer utility from the consumption of that output. This can be illustrated by a '**utility frontier**'. It is drawn on the assumption that production is efficient, that the economy is on the production possibility curve and that there are an infinite number of income (and hence, utility) distributions (see Figure 2).

Every point on the frontier is Pareto-efficient (one consumer can be made better-off only if the other is made worse-off), every point inside

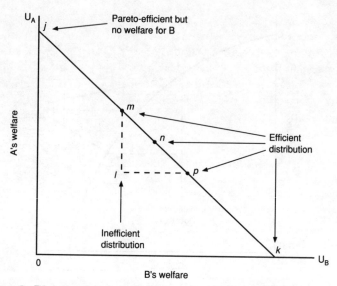

Figure 2 Distribution possibilities: maximum utility

it is inefficient. *l* is inefficient because it is possible to make A better-off without worsening B's position – a move to *m*, or to make B better-off without reducing A's welfare – a move to *p*; or, at *n*, both of them would be better-off. The inefficient situation exists when the two consumers value the two goods differently. If A values food more highly in terms of clothing than does B, and B values clothing in terms of food more highly than A, then if A gets more food (and less clothing), and B more clothing (and less food) the welfare of both is improved. When they both put the same value on food and clothing (in terms of the alternative good forgone), distributive efficiency is achieved. Points to the left of *m* or to the right of *p* are Pareto-efficient (Pareto-'optimal') though they appear to be unfair distributions of welfare. Even *j* is Pareto-efficient, though there B's utility is zero. The distribution problem would soon be solved by B's death. There would then be a Robinson Crusoe (before Friday) economy with only the *what?* and *how?* questions to be solved, and with the only criterion for judging the outcome that of efficiency.

Equity

Equity is about **social justice** and fairness, distributional goals. In terms of Figure 2, it requires people to make judgements about what points on the welfare frontier are desirable or acceptable. It requires us to evaluate policy changes which improve some people's welfare at the cost of reducing others'. For example, how much should people be taxed in order to provide others with goods or incomes? What point on the utility frontier is fair between A and B? It comes from a set of principles about what people ought to have *as of right*. However, this does not take us very far as different people have different principles; value judgements are involved.

A person taking an individualistic libertarian approach (see the box *Free to Choose overleaf*) would argue that equity is achieved if minimum standards – for income, education, health care, and so on – are achieved. This is to regard higher standards as part of society's reward system. Those with a fraternal, collectivist philosophy are

"I'll be glad when we have a classless society - I never could stand the poor."

not satisfied with minimum standards. What is fair for them is income support which takes account of the average standard, and equality of access to services such as health and education, and treatment according to need. If this erodes incentives (either of taxpayers or of claimants) there will be conflicts with efficiency. We will look at this in Chapter 7 on taxes and in Chapter 8 on poverty.

Free to choose

That different concept (as compared with 'equality before God' and equality of opportunity), equality of outcome, has been gaining ground in this century. In some intellectual circles the desirability of equality of outcome has become an article of religious faith: everyone should finish the race at the same time. As the Dodo said in *Alice in Wonderland*, '*Everybody* has won, and *all* must have prizes'.

For this concept, as for the other two, 'equal' is not to be interpreted literally as 'identical'. No one really maintains that everyone, regardless of age or sex or other physical qualities, should have identical rations of each separate item of food, clothing, and so on. The goal is rather 'fairness', a much vaguer notion – indeed, one that is difficult, if not impossible, to define precisely. 'Fair shares for all' is the modern slogan that has replaced Karl Marx's 'To each according to his needs, from each according to his ability'.

This concept of equality differs radically from the other two. Government measures that promote personal equality or equality of opportunity enhance liberty; government measures to achieve 'fair shares for all' reduce liberty. If what people get is to be determined by 'fairness', who is to decide what is 'fair'? As a chorus of voices asked the Dodo, 'But who is to give the prizes?'. 'Fairness' is not an objectively determined concept once it departs from identity. 'Fairness', like 'needs', is in the eye of the beholder. If all are to have 'fair shares', someone or some group of people must decide what shares are fair – and they must be able to impose their decisions on others, taking from those who have more than their 'fair' share and giving to those who have less. Are those who make and impose such decisions equal to those for whom they decided? Are we not in George Orwell's *Animal Farm*, where 'all animals are equal, but some animals are more equal than others'?

In addition, if what people get is determined by 'fairness' and not by what they produce, where are the 'prizes' to come from? What incentive is there to work and produce? How is it to be decided who is to be the doctor, who the lawyer, who the garbage collector, who the street sweeper? What assures that people will accept the roles assigned to them and perform those roles in accordance with their abilities? Clearly, only force or the threat of force will do.

Source: *Free to Choose* by Milton and Rose Friedman

The Friedmans' views are extreme, and their claim that 'equality of outcome' is the alternative to their ideas caricatures serious alternatives. Those who take a more fraternal view of society might argue for equality of access, and hence perhaps equality of outcome, to state-provided income in kind like health care and education. But no-one proposes equality of outcome in the provision of money incomes. There may be differences over what the level of cash support should be for those who need it, but there is no call for equal incomes for all.

Efficiency and equity are the criteria by which economic outcomes may be judged. In theory there is no problem over the definition of efficiency, though in practice there may be. Both in theory and in practice there are problems and disagreements over equity. This is because, as Lewis Carroll pointed out, 'the more there is of mine the less there is of yours'. Nevertheless the idea is used, along with efficiency, to judge how well real economies perform. This is the task we turn to in Chapter 3, after first having described alternative economic systems.

KEY WORDS

Allocation (what? how?)   Technical efficiency
Distribution (for whom?)   Allocative efficiency
Efficiency   Pareto efficiency
Equity   'Pareto optimum'
Welfare economics   Production possibility curve
Social welfare   Utility frontier
Normative   Social justice

Reading list

Anderton, A., *Economics*, Causeway Press, 1991, Units 33 and 41.

Beardshaw, J., Chapter 25 in *Economics: A Student's Guide*, 3rd edn, Pitman, 1992.

Friedman, M., and Friedman, R., Chapters 1 and 5 in *Free to Choose*, Penguin Books, 1980.

Hahn, F., 'Reflections on the invisible hand', *Lloyds Bank Review*, April 1982.

Wales, J., Chapter 10 in *Investigating Social Issues*, Macmillan, 1990.

Essay topics

1. Explain the distinction between wealth and welfare. Discuss whether or not increases in average earnings provide a suitable indication of increases in welfare. (Joint Matriculation Board, A/S level, 1990)

2. What is meant by an optimal allocation of resources? Under what conditions might market forces result in an optimal allocation of resources? (Associated Examining Board, 1989)

3. What is meant by the term 'economic efficiency'? To what extent does the price mechanism ensure that resources are allocated efficiently? (University of London Examinations and Assessment Council, 1990)

Data Response Question 1

Production possibilities

Suppose that ten individuals are shipwrecked on an isolated tropical island, on which there are two natural sources of food, coconuts and fish. Suppose that with their initial capital equipment each individual can collect two coconuts or catch one fish per hour.

1. Assuming that initially it is agreed that each individual should work for ten hours per day, illustrate the daily production possibility curve for coconuts and fish for this economy.
2. Why is the form of the production possibility curve different from the usual concave curve typically portrayed in economics textbooks?
3. Suppose that, after some time, a new tree climbing technique is discovered which makes it possible for an individual to collect four coconuts per hour. How would this discovery shift the production possibility curve?
4. Suppose that, following the introduction of the new climbing technique, the economy is observed to be producing 50 fish and 150 coconuts. Does this observation imply that the economy is producing at an inefficient point?
5. Suppose that, alternatively, it was assumed that out of the ten workers, five could collect coconuts but were incapable of catching fish, while the other five could catch fish but were incapable of collecting coconuts. Assuming, again, that the five workers in each activity were equally productive, what would the production possibility curve look like in this case, and what are the implications for the costs of production of coconuts in terms of fish?

(Welsh Joint Education Committee, 1989)

Chapter Two
Economic systems

'Would you tell me, please, which way I ought to go from here?'
'That depends a good deal on where you want to get to', said the
Cheshire Cat.   Lewis Carroll

Markets and planning

The mechanism by which resources are allocated to the production of output and by which output is distributed to final buyers is known as the **economic system**. The system comprises an organization or set of institutions: free markets constitute one such system, planning offices operating with a central planning bureau constitute another. Thus, economic systems can vary from, at one extreme, an unplanned free **market system** to, at the other extreme, a centrally planned **command economy**. Neither of these extremes is to be found in the real world because both systems have their drawbacks and weaknesses. *No economy relies entirely on the market, and no economy has central planners to take every single decision on what, how and for whom to produce.* A spectrum of systems with different degrees of planning and free market mechanisms exists; the economic system reflects the culture and values of the society it serves.

Ownership systems: capitalism and socialism

Capitalism refers to the private ownership of an economy's productive resources, **socialism** to social ownership. Under socialism the means of production are communally owned; for example, a factory may be owned by its workers, or, more usually, there is state ownership.

It is important to distinguish between an economy's *economic system* and its *ownership system*. Careless use of terms sees 'capitalism' and 'market system' and, similarly, 'socialism' and 'planned economy' used as if they were synonymous. They are not. Market economies, based on competition, tend to be capitalist; and socialism, with its cooperative philosophy, and planning have tended to go together. But this is not inevitable. For example, during the Second World War the UK remained capitalist but became a command economy; the government decided what and how to produce, and a rationing system determined who would get those goods not aimed at the war effort. Conversely, some countries which until recently have been socialist have always used markets, to a greater or lesser degree, to allocate resources.

There is, however, an argument that for market economies to work there *must* be a capitalist ownership system; and that without the profit incentive for private owners (see on) markets will not lead to efficient, cost-minimizing outcomes. This argument has been advanced particularly in the context of prescribing how eastern European economies should be reformed. It is probably correct when applied to a wholly state-owned economy, but it is unlikely to be true of a mixed economy where public enterprise and its managers are judged by the standards of private enterprise. *It does not appear that one hundred per cent of productive resources must be privately owned for an economy to be efficient.*

Nevertheless most commentators would concede that to achieve efficiency eastern European economies require market forces and privatization, particularly of those sectors of the economy which can be competitive. However, it might also be concluded that caution and selectivity might yield better outcomes than a headlong stampede to privatize everything, including natural monopolies, immediately.

In practice, all economies are a mixture of markets and planning, and there may be a mixture of capitalism and socialism. The USA, for example, is primarily a market economy, but even there the state decides on the allocation of resources to defence, education, roads, and so on, and determines the distribution of incomes and health care to the old and the poor. Conversely, in planned economies markets may be given some role in directing production.

Capitalism and socialism may also be mixed, though the ownership system may be purer than the economic system. There may be pure socialism, with no private ownership of anything apart from personal possessions (an example is Albania, at least until recently); or there may be fairly pure capitalism, with private ownership of nearly all productive resources. There may also be a mixture. In France, for example, there is fairly wide state ownership, including of manufacturing companies like Renault. Until the privatization programme of the 1980s, the UK had a similarly mixed system.

The command economy

In a command (planned) economy the government takes all decisions about consumption and production – what to produce, and how, and who gets it. Consumers are not sovereign, planners decide what to produce. The central planners also attempt to answer the *how?* question – they have to take decisions on production techniques and on the capital and labour intensity of production. For developed economies, the task is immensely complicated, even if aided by the most advanced of computers. Planners also determine income distribution. In a pure command economy money would not be necessary – people would receive pieces of paper giving direct entitlement to a particular quantity of specified goods and services. However, in practice, people receive money incomes which they are free to spend on those goods the planners have decided should be produced.

Planning failure

Planning, as compared with the invisible hand of free markets, has frequently been criticized for its inefficiency – in the general and the economic sense of that word. The failure of planned economies to achieve productive efficiency and to meet consumers' wants, and the recent changes in many of those economies towards the use of markets to allocate resources, shows that such criticism was well-founded. The view that planning can work as efficiently as decentralized markets has been fundamentally undermined.

The principal criticisms of the allocation of resources by planners are that production is not guided by consumer preferences, and that resources are not used in least-cost (most efficient) combinations. First, prices do not guide supply as they do in a market economy; they merely are raised or lowered to ration out what is produced. Planners may be guided to move resources because there are gluts or shortages or long order books. But the consumer can hardly be said to be sovereign. People get used to being grateful if they can find meat to buy, though really they might prefer fish. The inefficiency of planning in meeting consumer wants becomes a particular problem as an economy develops. In Maoist China, when everyone wore an identical blue uniform, it was not difficult to plan clothing output. But economic development brings a proliferation of products, so that there are millions of different goods and services. How would a planner know how many single-serving vegetable lasagnes or colourfast orchid lipsticks to produce? (An anti-growth person might argue that these are floss and fripperies. They appear, however, to be what people want. Fortunately discussion of economic systems and individual freedoms is beyond the scope of this book.)

Even if there were only thousands rather than millions of goods, the task of coordination of production would be complex because the output of one industry represents the inputs of many others. In a capitalist market economy, firms compete with each other to make profits, and in competitive markets the profit maximization motive leads them to use least-cost methods of satisfying consumers' wants. In a planned economy, competition and the motivation to make profits are absent, despite the use of 'notional' profits. Plant managers have to reach output targets, and receive bonuses for doing so, but there is little incentive for cost minimization. Targets depend on past production, and so for a margin of safety for the future, a plant manager will keep output below capacity potential. This is inefficient. There is further waste and expense in a planning system because there is a whole hierarchy of planners (civil servants, officials) who are unavailable for other more productive work. These are the people whose jobs depend on the existence of a planning system, the people who hindered *perestroika* (restructuring) in the former USSR.

Finally, planned economies can answer the *for whom?* question potentially satisfactorily. They can be fair, there need be no-one without an income, as there is in the market economy. However, planners do not have complete freedom to distribute goods. If people are to be motivated to do all the jobs that need doing, there have to be differentials between wage incomes. But these necessary differentials need not be as great as in a market system where some differences have non-economic causes. And the large inequalities which come from property ('unearned') income will not exist if the planned economy is also socialist. Income may be more equally distributed, but average income per head may be so much less than in more efficient market economies, that the poorest, though not so far from those with average or high incomes, may still be worse off than the poor in a market system. Whether the poor in a socialist command economy feel worse or better off than the poor in capitalist market systems depends on whether they assess their position in absolute or relative terms. There is an apocryphal story of an East German's view on the triumph of markets and capitalism: 'We only had Trabants then, but at least we all only had Trabants'. (Chapter 8 has something to say about relative poverty.)

The market economy

The decision-taking units in the market economy are households, who are resource owners and consumers, and firms, who are resource users and producers. Economic agents pursue their own interests. We assume that consumers aim at maximizing their own welfare or utility, and that firms aim at maximizing profits. The government plays no part in resource allocation and distribution in a pure market economy. Prices transmit information, are incentives to action, coordinate demand and supply, and distribute income.

Figure 3 shows a model of this system. Markets and prices allocate resources and distribute output. There is private ownership of resources, so it is also a capitalist as well as a market economy. Households and firms meet in the goods and factor markets. In the goods market the interaction of demand and supply determines prices, and prices inform firms what to produce. In the factor market, supply and demand determine wages, interest and rent, and these factor prices guide profit-maximizing firms to the least-cost (most efficient) combination of factors. The *how?* part of the allocation question is answered.

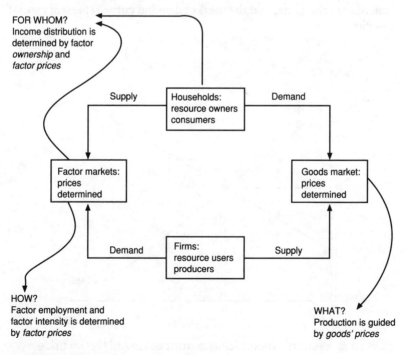

Figure 3 The market economy

Finally, distribution (*for whom?*): in a market economy a household's income depends on the factors it owns and the prices put on those resources in the factor market.

The price mechanism can achieve efficient – welfare-maximizing – levels of output. Figure 4 shows how this happens in the market for a single good. However, this is the result only if there is **perfect competition** and no **external effects**. For the moment we will assume that this is the situation.

Figure 4 shows market supply and demand curves obtained by summing firms' supply curves and consumers' demand curves. The supply curve of a firm in perfect competition is its marginal cost curve and the market supply curve is the sum of firms' MC curves (S = ΣMC). The market demand curve is the sum of individual's demand curves which reflect the welfare, or benefit, obtained from consumption (D = ΣMB). To find the optimum output for society we need to compare all the costs of production with all the benefits from consumption; that is, we need to compare **social costs** and **social benefits**. If there are no external effects (see on) then private costs and social costs are identical and the market supply curve represents social costs; similarly private and social benefits are the same, and the market demand curve represents social benefits.

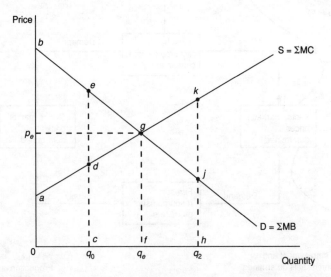

Figure 4 Welfare-maximizing output achieved by the price mechanism

Now we are in a position to see how the price mechanism achieves efficiency. For welfare to be maximized – for an efficient outcome – every unit which yields a larger benefit than it costs should be produced, and no unit which costs more than the benefits it provides should be made. This is the case at the market equilibrium, q_e. Each unit between o and q_e adds more to benefits than to costs. For example, the unit at q_0 costs cd but gives benefits of ce, so it adds de to net benefits. Every unit beyond (to the right of) q_e costs more than the benefits it yields. For example, if the marginal unit at q_2 were produced it would give benefits of hj but would cost much more, hk. Production should stop at q_e where marginal social cost and marginal social benefit (= fg) are exactly equal to each other. At the market equilibrium, achieved by price p_e, total benefits are $obgf$ and total costs are $oagf$; net benefits, abg, are maximized. **Allocative efficiency** is achieved.

How competitive markets achieve **productive efficiency** (cost minimization), which is part of an efficient outcome, will be shown in Chapter 3 when perfect competition is compared with monopoly.

Finally, the **distributive efficiency** illustrated in Figure 2 is also achieved by competitive markets. All consumers face the same set of prices. This leads each of them to get the same value (at the margin) from one good in terms of another. Within a given income distribution consumer welfare is maximized – the utility frontier is attained.

Market failure

The market achieves a welfare maximizing (efficient) outcome only when competition is perfect and when there are no external benefits or costs. Frequently this is not the case and the consequence is **market failure**. In the real world transactors may have incomplete information and their access to markets may be limited. Where there is monopoly there is no supply curve based on costs, profit maximizing output is less that efficient output, and some units which would add more to benefits than to costs are not produced (see Chapter 3). External effects also prevent the market from maximizing welfare. These effects happen when a good places costs or benefits on people not involved in its production or consumption. Pollution is an example of an external cost; protection from disease arising from another's immunization is an external benefit. When there are external costs (see Chapter 4) the supply curve does not include all costs. The supply curve is the sum of marginal private (firms') costs ($S = \Sigma MPC$), but marginal social costs (MSC), which include external costs, are greater. Because costs, and so price, are lower than if all costs were borne internally, output is extended beyond the efficient level, and some units are produced which add more to social costs than to benefits. Conversely, when there are external benefits (see Chapter 5), the demand curve does not reflect all societies' benefits from the consumption of a good, and there is under-production. Pure public goods may be regarded as an extreme case of external effects – all their benefits are external and they are not produced at all.

The failure of the market to provide incomes for all does not represent an efficiency failure. It is a failure to meet the distributional goal, however defined. There can be very different definitions of equity, but the fact that there are differences on how much redistribution there should be does not preclude agreement that some redistribution is necessary. The efficiency and equity problems that arise over redistribution are discussed in Chapter 8. In order to correct market failure the public sec-

---

Understanding how the markets operate

Sir, The Labour Party's new policy document declares that "the market can be a good servant, but is often a bad master." Your editorial comment ("Labour and the economy," May 21) disagrees.

You assert that "a market is not an imposition upon the people; it is a name for exchange among them. If the market is a servant, so are the people – and the government is the master."

In these words you reveal not only a fundamental misunderstanding of how market economies actually operate, but also a woeful ignorance of the basic principles of economics.

A competitive market economy is not an aggregation of mutual contracts between people ("a name for exchange among them"), but an autonomous mechanism, operating outside the control of individual participants. As François Quesnay, the founder of modern economies, wrote in 1756, the market operates "independent of men's will."

That is why the subject of economics exists at all. Its role is to explain how that market mechanism actually works, how a myriad of individual deci-

sions taken only in the light of market signals are coordinated by the invisible hand.

Proving the outcome to be efficient, even in some limited sense, requires mathematical assumptions too incredible to merit discussion – other than to point to the reality of market failure.

The elementary analysis of market failure suggests that, left to itself, the market will not ensure the socially desirable level of investment in education, in research, in infrastructure, or in the environment. In these cases the market is clearly a bad master.

And when next he is forced to modify his policies by the censure of the money markets, I am afraid that Mr Major will not be comforted by your belief that "if the market is a servant . . . government is the master."

The FT should catch up with a modern understanding of what markets are about – or at least catch up with the economics of 1756.

John Eatwell,
Trinity College,
Cambridge

Reader's letter, *FT*, May 1990

tor must get control over resources. It does this by imposing taxes, and in Chapter 7 taxes are assessed on how efficient and how fair they are.

The box *Understanding how markets operate* contains the reply of a reader (an economist) to a *Financial Times* leading article which showed little comprehension of how a market system operates. He explains the autonomous coordinating role of the market and points to the reality of market failure.

The mixed economy

In terms of resource allocation (*what? how?*), central planning fails fairly comprehensively. Markets are more successful, but they too mis-allocate resources and leave some people without incomes. A planned economy fails, but a market economy needs some planning. In the real world, economic systems are mixed. Following the collapse of the east European and Soviet systems there seems to be some convergence for developed economies towards what is primarily a market system. The price mechanism allocates resources, but a government sector inter-venes where the market fails. Thus the public sector's function is to produce public goods, control monopoly, and change resource alloca-tion by regulation and by taxes and subsidies where external effects lead to over- and under-production. It also ensures that people have minimum incomes.

Economies are also mixed in terms of their ownership systems. Internationally, within mixed though principally capitalist economies the spirit of the age has been towards privatization – less mixture, more capitalism (see *Privatization and the Public Sector* by Bryan Hurl). The formerly planned and socialist economies of eastern Europe (Poland, Hungary, etc.) are, at faster or slower rates, and with more or less success, moving both to markets and, via privatization, to capitalism. The peoples of the states which constituted the USSR want to follow the same path. The problems of transition are enormous, and those who have lived under the privations of planning probably have too rosy a view of what a market system can do, and of the merits of capitalism.

But in terms of the 'what to produce' and 'how to produce it' deci-sions the human mind has not been able to invent anything to match the market's ability to satisfy consumers' wants, and to do so effi-ciently. Provided that this fact does not blind us to its specific inefficien-cies and to its inequities, we should join Adam Smith in admiration of the working of the invisible hand. In the chapters which follow we dis-cover where it gets things wrong and what can be done about it.

```
                         KEY WORDS

    Economic system              Social costs
    Market system                Social benefits
    Command economy              Allocative efficiency
    Capitalism                   Productive efficiency
    Socialism                    Distributive efficiency
    Perfect competition          Market failure
    External effects             Mixed economy
```

Reading list

The Economist Brief, Chapter 8 in *Europe, the Revolution of 1989–92*.

Healey, N., and Levačić R., Chapters 3 and 4 in *Supply Side Economics*, 2nd edn, Heinemann Educational, 1992.

McCormick, B., 'The Market, a cause for regret?' *Economic Review*, November, 1992.

Paisley, R., and Quillfeldt, J., Exercises 2 and 28 in *Economics Investigated*, vol. 2, Collins Educational, 1992.

Whynes, D., Chapter 2 in *Welfare State Economics*, Heinemann Educational, 1992.

Essay topics

1. Explain what is meant by an 'economic system' and discuss the main criteria for distinguishing between types of economic system. Explain whether or not, in your view, recent events in eastern Europe confirm that the market mechanism provides the best approach to the problems of running national economies. (Joint Matriculation Board, 1992)

2. How are resources allocated in a mixed economy? In the light of the economic changes that have occurred within the United Kingdom in recent years, discuss whether it is still correct to describe the UK economy as a mixed economy. (Associated Examining Board, 1990)

3. What distinguishes a command economy from a free market economy? What problems arise in assessing the comparative performance of two such economies? (University of London Examinations and Assessment Council, 1991)

4. Why might the market mechanism not produce results which would satisfy the planner? (Oxford and Cambridge Examinations Board, 1991)

5. 'Most countries have a mixed economy; the only debate is about the strength of the mixture.' (Sir A. Cairncross) (a) What is meant by 'a mixed economy'? (b) Examine the above statement with respect to the problem of determining what should be 'the strength of the mixture'. (University of London Examinations and Assessment Council)

Data Response Question 2

Production quotas

At various times governments have adopted agricultural policies which impose restrictions on the land acreage which farmers can devote to the production of certain crops. In the UK, for example, the acreage which farmers could use to grow potatoes has been restricted.

However, such a policy has been criticized by agricultural economists on the grounds that in the long run it can result in productive inefficiency (i.e. given outputs are produced at above minimum costs). This criticism is based on consideration of the representative farmer's production function and the choice of production technique (i.e. the combination of land and other inputs used to produce crops). Figure A illustrates the situation of a representative farmer.

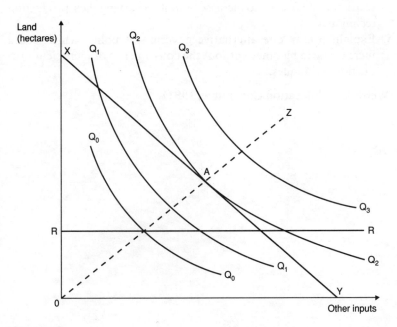

Figure A

In the diagram, Q_0Q_0, Q_1Q_1 etc. are isoquants, indicating the output of potatoes that can be produced with different input combinations. The line XY is an iso-cost line, the slope of which indicates the relative price of land in terms of other inputs such as labour, machinery, fertilizers, etc. The point A denotes the representative farmer's choice of outputs and inputs *before* acreage restrictions are imposed. The line RR shows the maximum acreage of land that an individual farmer can use *after* the acreage restriction imposed by the government. Answer the following questions, explaining your reasoning.

1. Suppose farmers in the short run are restricted to the production technique shown by the dotted line 0Z. What quantity of output will be produced when the acreage restriction is imposed?
2. Suppose that in the longer run production techniques can be varied. With reference to the diagram, indicate how farmers can increase output while still observing the acreage restriction.
3. Suppose farmers, still observing the acreage restriction, increase output to the level shown by isoquant Q_2Q_2. Explain why the cost of producing this output is higher than it was before the acreage restriction was imposed.
4. Consider the impact on the consumer of the policy of acreage restriction if farmers do increase output by varying their production techniques.
5. Explain briefly *one* alternative government policy which could increase farm incomes without the consequence of inefficient production techniques.

(Welsh Joint Education Committee, 1991)

Chapter Three
Monopoly and competition: theory

'You've no right to grow here', said the Dormouse.   Lewis Carroll

Markets can be characterized in terms of

- the numbers of buyers and sellers, and
- the nature of the product which is bought and sold.

The efficiency of markets depends on the degree to which market prices reflect the costs of supply, on the one hand, and the preferences and satisfaction of the consumer on the other. For market prices to be sensitive to these influences, firms have to compete through price in both selling products and buying factors and be unable to dominate either other firms or consumers. The degree of price competition can, however, vary widely from zero to infinity.

In perfect **monopoly** a good is sold by a single seller and there are **barriers to entry** which prevent new firms from joining the industry to supply the market.

At the other extreme, **perfect competition** exists in markets where there are many firms all selling an identical (homogeneous) product and where there is **freedom of entry** for new firms.

In each case the decision-makers do not have to bother about the effects of their decisions on other firms. In the first case there are none, and in the second case each firm is so small that, if it went out of business or doubled its output, it would have a negligible effect on market supply.

These two types of market structure define the extremes of a scale of price competition and are less commonly found in the real world. More common market structures comprise different numbers of firms of different sizes whose behaviour shows some degree of price competition but which also may have some of the characteristics of monopoly. The degree of **market power** is measured by the **concentration ratio**, which shows the percentage of sales held by the industry's largest firms. The four-firm or eight-firm concentration ratio is often cited. An example of considerable market power would be a 60 per cent four-firm concentration ratio.

An industry dominated by a few large firms whose behaviour is interdependent, is an **oligopoly**. In oligopoly each firm has a significant share of total sales so that one firm's price and output decisions will affect the sales of its rivals. What it decides to do therefore depends on how it thinks its rivals will react; there is uncertainty. Profits would be higher if firms got together to agree to cut output and to raise price – that is, to reduce uncertainty by acting as if they were a monopoly. Thus **collusion** can take place, usually covertly (because it is illegal), in order to fix price and output at levels to create extra (monopoly) profits.

The use of market power to distort prices and output from what they would have been under competitive equilibrium results in a reallocation of resources and a reduction in economic welfare. In what follows we shall evaluate the implications of competition and monopoly for the efficiency and equity of resource allocation. In the next chapter we review government policy toward monopoly.

Competition and efficiency

Figure 4 in Chapter 2 shows that allocative efficiency is achieved if output and price are set where the market demand and supply curves intersect. This is on the assumption that there are no externalities so that the supply curve represents all costs to society of producing the good (social cost); and that the consumers' benefits which give the demand curve represent all the benefits society obtains from consuming it (social benefit). For this ideal allocation to be achieved all markets in the economy must be perfectly competitive.

Under perfect competition, where there are large numbers of competing firms, the output of any one firm is such a small proportion of the total that any change in a single firm's output will have no effect on market price. This price is determined in the market for the good. Here the market supply curve is the sum of all firms' supply curves (which are their marginal cost curves) and the market demand curve is the sum of all consumers' demand curves (which are their marginal benefit curves). Price and output are set where market demand and supply curves intersect.

The situation is the same as that depicted in Figure 4 (p.16) which shows **allocative efficiency**. If every industry and market were perfectly competitive (and if there were no external effects) then a market economy would achieve allocative efficiency.

Perfect competition also achieves **productive efficiency** – output at minimum resource cost. This requires that all firms produce at minimum average costs, and that all firms' costs are the same. We will now see how this happens. The competitive firm is a **price-taker** and the

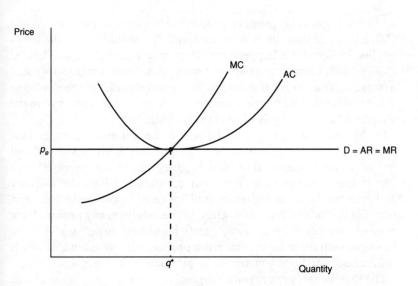

Figure 5 The long-run equilibrium of the perfectly competitive firm

price set in the market gives each firm its demand curve. This is the perfectly elastic, horizontal, schedule at the ruling market price shown in Figure 5.

The perfectly elastic demand schedule shows that whatever quantity (up to the limit of its capacity) a firm puts on the market, the price is unaffected. If it attempted to get a higher price it would sell nothing, and as a **profit maximizer** it would not charge lower than the market price. The schedule shows the price at which all units may be sold – this is the average revenue obtained for each unit, and it is also the revenue received for each additional unit sold (marginal revenue). Hence we may label the curve: demand (D), average revenue (AR), and marginal revenue (MR). The firm's average and marginal cost curves (AC and MC) are also shown. **Normal profits**, the opportunity costs or returns necessary to keep resources producing this good rather than another, are included in the firm's costs.

The firm is in equilibrium when it maximizes profits, or minimizes losses. This happens when it produces every unit of output which adds more to revenue than to costs. This means that it will produce every unit up to that marginal one which costs as much to produce (MC) as it adds to revenue (MR). In Figure 5, q^* is the profit-maximizing output level, where MC = MR. To the left of q^*, MC < MR so that units produced over this range add to the firm's profits; to the right of q^* each additional unit costs more to produce (MC) than it adds to revenue (MR); if any of these units were produced they would reduce the firm's profits. In Figure 5 it happens that at q^* where profits are maximized (MC = MR), average costs are at a minimum, and average costs equal average revenue – only normal profits are being made. We then need to ask if this is what we should expect to be the case. The answer is: in the short-run 'not necessarily', but in the long-run 'yes'.

In the short-run, price may be above the minimum average cost and above-normal profits will result. Output (where MC = MR = p) will be at a level above that which gives minimum average cost. But if this happens new firms will be attracted into the industry and price will be competed down until it is equal to average revenue and only normal profits are made. Thus, in the long-run, any profits above normal are competed away and high-cost firms go out of business, with the result that output is produced at minimum cost which is the same in all firms and maximum productive efficiency is achieved.

The firm's supply curve is its marginal cost curve. The marginal cost curve shows what quantity will be supplied at any price. The market supply curve is then the sum of the firms' supply or marginal cost curves (ΣMC). The market demand curve is the sum of the individual demand curves which show consumer benefits (ΣMB). Thus in perfect competition (and when there are no externalities), the supply curve shows the cost to society of each extra unit and the demand curve shows the benefits it provides. Output is at that point which maximizes welfare because only those units which provide more benefit than cost are produced, and firms are guided to produce at minimum cost. If this were the state of affairs over the whole of the economy, then there would be maximum output from the economy's resources, and maximum benefit to consumers from that output. Perfect competition would achieve Pareto efficiency (see Chapter 1).

Monopoly and efficiency

Under monopoly, which restricts output to achieve higher prices, some output which would add more to benefits than to costs is not produced. If we assume that costs are the same whether an industry operates under perfect competition or under monopoly (we will later drop this assumption), then monopoly output is lower and price is higher than under perfect competition. We assume the extreme monopoly case; a single firm producing all output. The firm is the industry and faces the downward sloping market demand curve (Figure 6).

The schedule shows that the monopoly firm can set either price or quantity but not both. If the firm sets the price for example at p_1, then

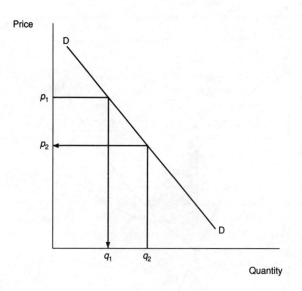

Figure 6 The demand curve of the monopoly firm

the demand curve shows the quantity which will be bought, which is q_1. Or, if the firm puts a certain quantity on the market, then the price will be what the market will bear; for example if q_2 is offered for sale then the price must be p_2.

To increase sales the price must be reduced. It is not only the marginal buyer who will pay the lower price, but also those buyers already in the market who were paying the higher price. This means that when quantity sold is increased by a price reduction the addition to total revenue (marginal revenue) is not equal to the price (average revenue) obtained for that extra unit. This happens because some revenue is lost from intra-marginal buyers previously paying the higher price. For this reason marginal revenue lies below average revenue.

Pareto efficiency will not be achieved under monopoly. Figure 7 on p.28 shows the demand curve facing the monopoly firm (D = AR) with its marginal revenue curve (MR) lying below, together with the average and marginal cost curves.

The monopoly firm which aims to maximize profits will produce all those units which add more to revenue than to cost. Up to a each unit provides the firm with more revenue than it costs to produce (MR > MC); beyond a each unit costs the firm more to produce than it adds to revenue (MC > MR). A profit-maximizing firm will therefore produce q_m, the quantity shown at a (where MC = MR); and the demand curve shows that q_m can be sold at price p_m.

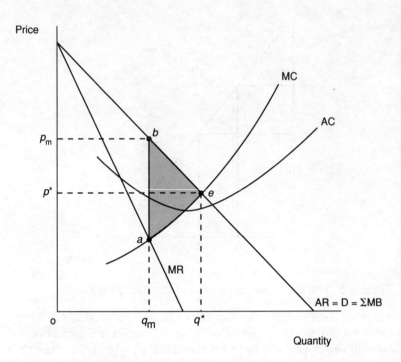

Figure 7 Price and output under monopoly

This outcome is not allocatively efficient because resources are not allocated to produce some units of the good whose value to consumers is higher than their marginal cost of production. Pareto efficiency is not achieved. At q_m the marginal unit adds $q_m b$ to consumer welfare, but costs only $q_m a$ to produce. Units to the right of q_m are also valued more highly by consumers (shown by the demand curve) than they would cost to produce (MC curve). This is the case for each unit up to q^*, the optimal output where marginal costs and benefits are equal. The total loss of welfare arising from monopoly is the loss from not producing each potential unit of output between q and q^*. These would all add more to society's benefits than they would cost society to produce, but they remain unproduced because each one would involve the monopolist in a net loss of revenue. The **deadweight loss** from monopoly is shown by the shaded area *abe*. It arises because resources are allocated inefficiently – they are not used where there would be net welfare gains. If the monopoly were broken up into small units, the marginal cost curve (now the sum of many firms' marginal costs) would be the supply curve. Equilibrium would be at e where the demand and supply curves intersect. Price would be p^* and output would be at the efficient level, q^*.

Figure 7 shows that, as well as being allocatively inefficient, monopoly is also productively inefficient. At output q_m average costs are still falling production is not at minimum average cost.

Monopoly and income distribution: consumer exploitation

As well as being inefficient, monopoly is inequitable. There is **consumer exploitation**. By restricting output and charging a higher price than in perfect competition, a firm with monopoly power extracts **monopoly profits**. It is likely that these profits go to well-off owners at the expense of less well-off consumers. It seems not unreasonable to regard redistribution of income by the rich to the rich as unfair.

In Figure 8, monopoly profits are shown as the difference (at output q_m) between total revenue ($op_m bq_m$) and total cost ($odcq_m$). They are represented by the shaded rectangle $dp_m bc$. As pure monopoly has been defined as a single firm supplying all output, with no competitors and with barriers to entry so that competitors are excluded, monopoly profits (above normal, or super-normal, profits) will persist into the long-run.

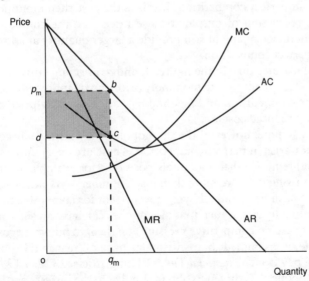

Figure 8 Monopoly profits

Cartels

In the real world, monopolization of an industry by a single firm is far less likely than oligopoly. When competition is between a few firms it is in their interests, and it becomes possible for them, to collude to restrict output and to raise price in order to gain monopoly profits. When a group of firms overtly colludes on price and output it becomes a **cartel**. More than two hundred years ago Adam Smith warned of the propensity of businessmen to collude to raise their profits: 'People of the same trade seldom meet together, even for merriment and diversion, but the conversation ends in a conspiracy against the public or in some contrivance to raise prices' (*Wealth of Nations*). In most countries cartels are illegal. Collusion, which remains profitable, then becomes tacit or covert.

Is monopoly always bad?

Costs

The reasoning which showed that perfect competition produced a larger quantity at a lower price than monopoly was based on the assumption that costs would be the same whether output was supplied by a large number of small firms or by a single seller. This assumption is unlikely to be the case in the real world. It is more probable that a monopolist would achieve **economies of scale** which would make costs lower than in perfect competition. If this is the case then monopoly, despite the restriction of output to raise price, and the consequent allocative inefficiency, might still provide a larger quantity at a lower price than perfect competition.

Figure 9 illustrates this. In the figure, p_c and q_c are competitive price and quantity, p_{m1} and q_{m1} are monopoly price and quantity with costs as in perfect competition, and p_{m2} and q_{m2} are monopoly price and quantity with reduced costs.

We must also note, however, that monopolies may incur *some* costs which do not arise in perfect competition. These are expenditures to maintain and reinforce their monopoly position – for example 'institutional' advertising ('You're more than just a number' – BT advertising to domestic consumers) and lobbying government for favourable treatment. Additionally it is argued that monopolies can have an 'easy life' because there are no competitive pressures on them to minimize costs. For example, it is claimed that British Gas has not 'driven hard bargains on the pay front' (*Financial Times* leading article, 23 May 1991), nor do monopolies feel driven to obtain supplies at the lowest cost.

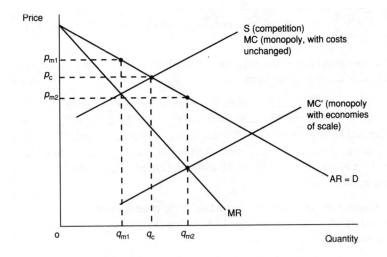

Figure 9 Lower costs in monopoly

Natural monopolies

'**Natural monopolies**' are an extreme case of the lower costs argument. A natural monopoly exists when average costs fall over a long range of output levels. If there are competing firms, the largest of the competitors will have the lowest costs and will force out the others. The larger it becomes (relative to the size of the market) the lower its average costs. Figure 10 in Chapter 4 depicts the natural monopoly.

Public utilities such as electricity supply, gas supply and water are all examples of natural monopolies. Overlapping local distribution systems would make no sense and would increase costs. In some natural monopolies, though not the utilities listed above, technological change may make competition possible. With the development of electronic mail and satellite transmission, the telecommunications industry is an example.

Invention, innovation and economic growth

The other principal argument in favour of monopoly is that in a capitalist market economy it promotes economic growth and that the **dynamic gains** to society from the **innovation** undertaken by monopolistic firms far outweigh **static losses** arising from misallocation. This argument derives from a famous work, *Capitalism, Socialism and Democracy* (1942) by Joseph Schumpeter (see the box on p.32).

We have to ask if Schumpeter's argument is correct. Does society gain

Extracts from *Capitalism, Socialism and Democracy* by Joseph A. Schumpeter

The essential point to grasp is that in dealing with capitalism we are dealing with an evolutionary process . . .

Capitalism is by nature a form or method of economic change and not only never is but never can be stationary . . . The fundamental impulse that sets and keeps the capitalist engine in motion comes from the new consumers' goods, the new methods of production or transportation, the new markets, the new forms of industrial organization that capitalist enterprise creates . . .

This process of Creative Destruction is the essential fact about capitalism. It is what capitalism exists in and what every capitalist concern has got to live in.

. . . restrictive (monopolistic) practices . . . acquire a new significance in the perennial gale of creative destruction, a significance which they would not have in a stationary state . . .

. . . largest scale plans could in many cases not materialize at all if it were not known from the outset that competition will be discouraged by heavy capital requirements or lack of experience, or that means are available to discourage or checkmate it so as to gain the time and space for further developments . . .

What we have got to accept is that (monopoly power) has come to be the most powerful engine of (economic) progress and in particular of the long-run expansion of total output not only in spite of, but to a considerable extent through, this strategy which looks so restrictive when viewed in the individual case and from the individual point of view . . . It is hence a mistake to base the theory of government regulation of industry on the principle that big business should be made to work as the respective industry would work in perfect competition.

Fourth Edition, pp 83–106

more from the dynamic power of monopoly and oligopoly in promoting economic growth than it loses from the misallocation of resources? The argument to support Schumpeter is that monopolies have both the ability (high profits) and the incentive (potential future profits which will not be competed away) to undertake the **research and development** which lead to **new processes** and **new products**. On the other hand, monopolists can survive even if they do not undertake these activities as they are insulated from competitive pressures. However, in most industries monopoly power is shared by a few large firms which makes them feel less secure than would a single monopoly firm, and so such behaviour less likely. Even where there is a single monopoly firm it is not sheltered forever because in the long-run substitutes can be found for nearly every good and service. Perhaps water is the only exception to this. For example, if gas became extremely expensive and inefficiently serviced, people would gradually turn to electricity to heat their homes and cook their food.

In contrast, it can be argued that the ability and motivation for competitive firms to innovate is much less. They do not have the monopoly profits to spend on research and development, and if they achieve technical advance and develop a new product or a new process, other firms are free to enter their market and share their rewards. To reap the benefits of innovation an innovating firm needs monopoly power. Governments give such monopoly power, for a certain period of time, by the granting of **patents**. A patent is a temporary legal monopoly and its intention is to stimulate innovation in competitive markets by enabling inventors to recoup the rewards of their genius, hard work and luck. It appears that for medium to large-sized firms, patent laws which protect profits from innovation are effective incentives to research and development.

Studies which have attempted to discover whether the dynamic gains from monopoly outweigh the deadweight loss show (for the USA) results varying from losses valued at 0.1 per cent to losses of 13 per cent of GNP (the latter also including costs directed at maintaining monopoly power). In the next chapter we turn to look at monopoly policy and the assumptions on which it is based. The USA, for example, starts with the assumption that monopoly power is always bad – 'you've no right to grow here', as Lewis Carroll's Dormouse said. But UK policy is more pragmatic, balancing costs against benefits.

KEY WORDS

Monopoly	Consumer exploitation
Barriers to entry	Monopoly profits
Perfect competition	Cartel
Freedom of entry	Economies of scale
Market power	Natural monopolies
Concentration ratio	Public utilities
Oligopoly	Dynamic gains
Collusion	Innovation
Allocative efficiency	Static losses
Productive efficiency	Research and development
Price-taker	New products
Profit-maximizer	New processes
Normal profits	Patents
Deadweight loss	

Reading list

Anderton, A., *Economics*, Causeway Press, 1991, Unit 37.

Bennett, P., and Cave, M., Chapter 2 in *Competition Policy*, Heinemann Educational, 1991.

Beardshaw, J., Chapters 14, 17 and 18 in *Economics; A Student's Guide*, 3rd edn, Pitman, 1992.

Bibby, D., 'Efficiency in private and public sectors', *Economic Review*, Sept. 1992.

Maunder, P., Chapters 22–24 in *Economics Explained*, 2nd edn, Collins Educational, 1991.

Essay topics

1. Are there any advantages to monopoly and disadvantages to competition? Discuss what gains there might be, if any, from the abolition of the monopoly of the Post Office to collect and deliver letters. (Joint Matriculation Board, 1992)

2. What is meant by economic efficiency? Can monopolies ever be efficient? (Associated Examining Board, 1992)

3. 'Only large firms can exploit economies of scale. Economies of scale lead to lower costs. Lower costs lead to lower prices. Therefore, large firms are good for society.' Discuss. (University of Oxford Delegacy of Local Examinations, 1992)

4. What is meant by economic efficiency in the case of a single firm? What criteria could be used to estimate the extent to which a firm was economically efficient? (Oxford and Cambridge Schools Examination Board, 1990)

Data Response Question 3

The force of competition

This task is based on a question set by the University of London School Examinations Board (now the Examinations and Assessment Council) in 1990. Read the article, which is adapted from 'Cement splits to face the force of competition' by A. Jackson published in the *Times* on 13 February 1987, and answer the questions.

One of the oldest cartels in the country has been disbanded leaving British cement manufacturers to fight it out. Blue Circle Industries (the market leader with 56.5 per cent of the market share), Rugby Portland Cement and Rio Tinto Zinc will now be able to charge variable prices throughout the country. This was a reluctant decision on the part of the cartel.

The common price agreement has been in existence since 1934, the firms maintaining that it was in the public interest for cement prices to be fixed countrywide. However, faced with a declining market after the construction industry peak in 1973, the major cement manufacturers were vulnerable. A major reason for the decline in the construction industry after 1973 was cuts in public expenditure. Thus, while gross domestic product rose by 16 per cent over the period 1973–85, output of the construction industry fell by 15 per cent. By the late 1970s our excess capacity in Britain was accompanied by a surplus in the rest of the world. The British market became a perfect target for importers.

Another development has been the growth in the use of substitute materials or extenders. Blast furnace slag and pulverised fuel ash are the two materials which can be blended successfully with ordinary Portland cement without impairing its cementitious properties.

1. Why should the author suggest that the abandonment of the cement cartel was 'a reluctant decision' of UK cement manufacturers?
2. How might the cement manufacturers have argued that the cartel was in the public interest?
3. Using appropriate diagram(s), analyse the factors which caused cement manufacturers to become 'vulnerable' after 1973.

Chapter Four
Monopoly and competition: policy

'In that case', said the Dodo, 'I move that the meeting adjourn, for the immediate adoption of more energetic remedies.'   Lewis Carroll

---

The box below shows how restriction of output by a monopoly supplier (here, National Power, a privatized electricity generator) can raise price it is a clear illustration of why governments need to have policies to deal with monopoly power. Here it is a producer (rather than a consumer) who is exploited by the monopolist but the principle illustrated is general.

National Power's profits indicate need for prices investigation

Sir, With National Power's announcement of a staggering increase in profits of 18.1 per cent ("National Power reaches £202m", 27 November), it is high time to focus on the fixing of pool prices by the electricity generators. This is nothing short of a scandal. They should be investigated immediately by the Monopolies Commission.

Most big electricity consumers were forced to accept pool prices in order to avoid a 15 per cent increase in their electricity costs which was a consequence of taking the alternative annual contracts offered by the area boards. These pool prices are fixed every half hour on a supply and demand basis.

Traditionally, demand peaks in the later afternoon and, therefore, one expects the pool prices to be more expensive at this time. However, there is a limit to this and it is far below the levels recently experienced.

For example, for much of the day a pool price somewhere between 2p and 3p per unit tends to prevail, but on a number of days recently the late afternoon price has been as high as 11p. This has been on days when the weather has been mild and no extraordinary conditions have existed.

All indications are that the generators have deliberately withdrawn capacity during these periods in order to force prices up – in short, the market is being wilfully manipulated.

The regulatory authority OFFER, has shown itself to be completely spineless and responds to complaints from consumers such as me in a most negative fashion. Yet I am purchasing £6m worth a year of electricity, it is 8 per cent of my manufacturing costs and I find that these are being forced up well above 1990–91 levels as a result of this pricing practice.

The consequences of having to absorb these cost increases are potentially disastrous – it is already hard enough being competitive in these recessionary times, with overseas producers pushing to increase their market share.

The arcane and secretive way in which pool pricing is established, with the customer not getting to know the actual price he has paid until four weeks after he has consumed the electricity, also makes it impossible to plan and control costs.

Andrew Cook
Chairman, William Cook
Parkway Avenue
Sheffield

Source: *Financial Times*, 1991

The boxed extract 'Competition, not cahoots' shows that the problem lies not only with single-firm monopolies, but also with cartels where firms band together in order to extract monopoly profits. The extract also criticizes British competition policy which is further discussed in the next section.

Competition, not cahoots

Britain needs nastier penalties for cartels

The three widget-makers who control the British widget market sit down together over Beef Wellington and good claret and, in such hard times, agree to raise their prices by 20%. Widget-making is an expensive trade to get into, and so the price rise sticks. Widget shareholders rejoice. Widget purchasers complain, and the fearful shadow of Sir Gordon Borrie, director-general of the Office of Fair Trading, falls across the widget-makers' cabal. What vengeance will the law wreak? At most, a court order telling them not to do it again. They can keep their ill-gotten profits.

Britain's law against cartels offers too little incentive for virtue. True, the Restrictive Trade Practices Act sets out all sorts of agreements that companies may not make; but the law imposes no penalty on those who then proceed to make them. The OFT, the government body responsible for implementing the law, can do no more than get a court order to stop them repeating the offence. If they ignore that, they can be fined for contempt of court. So last year a cartel of concrete companies was fined (all of £20,000–25,000 each) for fixing prices because they had been caught out doing the same thing five years earlier. But others tackled by the OFT – in insurance, glass, roofing, fuel oil and buses, for instance – have got off with a slap on the wrist.

Source: *The Economist*, 6 April 1991

Competition policy

In their **competition policy** governments seek efficiency and equity. Policies aim at minimizing the misallocation of resources caused by monopoly, and at preventing the exploitation of consumers. There are broadly two possible approaches: the first seeks to **break up** monopoly and to make it more like competitive industry; the second aims not to break up but to **regulate** it with permanent bodies to investigate and to oversee potential abusers of monopoly power.

The first approach has long been used in the USA, the second represents the British way. The American approach would appear to be based on the presumption that monopoly is necessarily bad, whereas the British attitude is more pragmatic – it judges each case on its merits and balances the gains from monopoly against the costs:

- economies of scale
- strength in international competition
- the efficiency of the particular firm
- research and development
- long-run growth

are set against:

- output restriction
- consumer exploitation
- lack of incentive to minimize costs.

"I hope we don't get broken up into a cartel"

On this basis the Monopolies and Mergers Commission (MMC) investigates cases referred to it by the Director General of Fair Trading who supervises competition and consumer law. However, as the extract 'Competition, not cahoots' showed, British policy against cartels can, in practice, be extremely feeble. British companies may also be caught by EC law, which is potentially more severe than even US law, but it applies only to international trade.

Policy and natural monopolies: nationalization, privatization and regulation

Figure 10 shows a natural monopoly such as electricity distribution where larger output leads to lower average costs. Over the whole range of output, marginal cost lies below average cost.

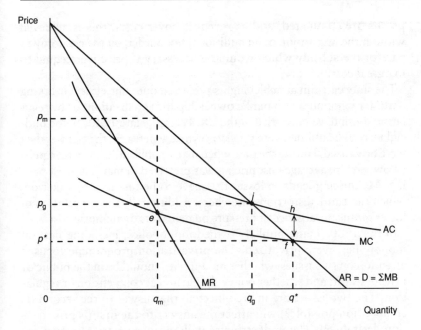

Figure 10 Pricing policies for a natural monopoly

Without regulation, equilibrium is at e where MC = MR. This leads to price p_m and output q_m and monopoly profits are made. This compares with the allocatively efficient output and price at p^* and q^* where MC = MB (given by the average revenue curve). At this output, price/average revenue (set equal to marginal cost) is below average cost so that losses are made.

To reduce or remove misallocation and exploitation of the consumer, public policy aims to increase output and reduce price. For Pareto efficiency, output should be at q^* with price p^*. The average loss, fh per unit sold, would be covered by a subsidy of fh per unit whether the firm were in the private or public sector. However, this outcome represents the ideal, or **first-best**, efficiency. It would be the outcome sought if everywhere in the economy price were set equal to marginal cost. However, if in most of the rest of the economy perfect competition does not prevail then a **second-best** solution might be recommended: output at j where average cost and average revenue are equal, with output q_g and price p_g. The principle of the second best means that if in the rest of the economy the first best outcome (MSC = MSB) does not hold then it is inefficient to enforce that outcome in a single sector. Though j is not the first best solution, output q_g is larger than in monopoly, monopoly profits are eliminated, and as revenues cover costs, this is achieved without the imposition of an additional tax burden on the economy to pay for the subsidy which would be necessary if price were equal to marginal cost.

The state can aim at achieving its preferred outcome either by taking natural monopolies into **public ownership (nationalization)** or by regulation. Both have been tried in the UK. From the late 1940s to the mid-eighties public utilities were publicly owned, whereas in the eighties they were privatized. During the time when many public utilities were in public ownership, average-cost pricing was preferred to marginal-cost pricing. MC pricing leads to losses that have to be financed by taxation, which can cause distortions elsewhere. Additionally the expectation of losses means the absence of pressure on managers to minimize costs.

In the 1980s many publicly owned monopolies, including natural monopolies, were privatized. The **privatization** programme focused attention on two issues: whether monopolies should be in the public or private sector, and whether policy should aim at competition or regulation. The two issues are interconnected: the answer to the second (is competition possible?) will affect the answer to the first (is privatization desirable?). The undoctrinaire will approve of privatization for industries where competition is feasible, but will prefer true monopolies to remain in public ownership.

The central issues, whether in public or private ownership, are cost minimization together with optimal output level (efficiency); and the protection of the consumer (equity). The conventional wisdom is that cost minimization is more likely in the private sector where the motivation to make profits is the driving force. (The experience of British Steel when still in public ownership in the early 1980s shows that efficiency gains can be made even without this). However, in the private sector protection for the buyer (which includes energy and water using firms as well as households) becomes more urgent as exploitation by profit maximizers becomes more likely. The letter at the start of this chapter showed the problem high prices pose for firms competing in world markets. For some public utilities break-up and hence competition is feasible, for example in telecommunication and in electricity generation. But natural monopolies, where competition is not feasible, persist: electricity and gas distribution to small consumers and water supplies within their own areas. In these circumstances regulation must protect consumers. The activity and the success of the regulators for each industry, OFFER, OFGAS and OFWAT, has varied. The principal means of regulation has been a formula for price increases 'RPI minus x', where the x per cent deducted from

"It's not a telephone – it's a profit maximisation module"

the Retail Price Index is set to take account of the potential for efficiency gains.

However monopoly profits continue: in 1991–92, a year of deep recession, privatized utilities' dividends grew by an average 10 per cent, which compared with an average increase of only 1 per cent for other (all-share) dividends. In referring to those effects a commentator wrote: 'The worry is that the creation of a profit conscious utility sector, ready to exploit its monopoly position for commercial gain, is doing serious harm to the competitiveness of the rest of the economy' (Barry Riley, *Financial Times*, June 1992).

The persistence of monopoly profits where competition is not possible, or where competition has not emerged because of high entry costs, causes commentators who approved of much of the privatization programme to have their doubts about privatizing public utilities. If cost reductions could be obtained in the public sector then many would have been happy to see the natural monopolies remain in public ownership.

However, the motivation and the ability of these enterprises, when in the private sector, to make monopoly profits is an object lesson to students of economics. 'More energetic remedies', as the Dodo recommended, are needed.

KEY WORDS

Competition policy	Second-best
Break up	Public ownership
Regulate	Nationalization
First-best	

Reading list

Bennett, P., and Cave, M., *Competition Policy*, Heinemann Educational, 1991.

Griffiths, A., UK restrictive trade practices, *British Economy Survey*, Longman, autumn 1992.

Hurl, B., *Privatization and the Public Sector*, 2nd edn, Heinemann Educational, 1992.

Paisley, R., and Quillfeldt, J., Module 27 in *Economics Investigated*, vol. 2, Collins Educational, 1992.

Essays topics

1. Explain how the economic efficiency of an industry may be affected by the existence of scale economies. Discuss whether or not the economic efficiency of the water and electricity supply industries is likely to be improved by privatization. (Joint Matriculation Board, 1990)

2. Analyse, with examples, the nature and likely benefits of economies of scale to large manufacturing companies. In the light of these benefits why does the government find it necessary to investigate industrial mergers? (University of Cambridge Local Examinations Syndicate, 1992)

3. Account for the growth in the number of referrals to the Monopolies and Mergers Commission since 1987. Does this trend suggest that competition policy is more, or less, effective than previously? (Oxford and Cambridge Schools Examination Board, 1991)

4. For what reasons do governments often seek to regulate monopolies and monopolistic agreements between firms? UK monopoly policy treats large-firm monopoly situations on an individual case-by-case basis, as opposed to outright prohibition. What arguments could support this policy? (Welsh Joint Education Committee, 1991)

Data Response Question 4

Competition and innovation in the European Community

This task is based on a question set by the Associated Examining Board in 1991. Read the article, which is adapted from an internal economic paper for the EC Commission ('Competition and innovation' by G. A. Geroski), and answer the questions.

1. Explain, in your own words, what the writer means by the terms: (i) dynamic efficiency, (ii) static efficiency, and (iii) monopoly power.

2. Explain why it seems reasonable to argue that: (i) 'increases in market size will increase innovation', and (ii) 'large firms with at least some degree of monopoly power are likely to be most innovative'.

3. Discuss the view that removing all barriers to trade within the EC will bring substantial gains to all member states.

There are a number of obstacles which restrict trade within the European Community, and there are good reasons to think that removing them may bring substantial gains to all member states. Policies have been suggested to tackle these problems, and if adopted they are likely to improve the allocation of resources within the EC.

The primary effects of reducing the barriers to trade between countries who are members of the EC will be an increase in market size and in the amount of competition in the enlarged market. These changes are likely to affect the efficiency of firms and the performance of markets in several different ways. When examining these effects, it is necessary to distinguish between dynamic efficiency and static efficiency.

Improvements in dynamic efficiency will result if the removal of barriers to trade leads to invention, innovation and a faster rate of technological change. However even if these long run benefits do not occur it is still almost certain that there will be improvements in static efficiency. A larger market and more competition is likely to result in a better allocation of resources, even if the pace of technological change in unaffected. The only controversy is about the size of the benefits which will result from these improvements in static efficiency.

A larger market and the resulting increase in demand will allow firms with unexploited economies of scale to move down their long run average cost curves. More competition is also likely to encourage firms to reduce inefficiency and to produce whatever output they choose, at the lowest average cost. These two effects lead to the prediction that costs are likely to fall as the size of the market and the degree of competition increase.

The effects of market size and competition on dynamic efficiency, however, are much less clear. Certainly it seems reasonable to suggest that increases in market size will increase innovation, particularly if there are any economies of scale or fixed costs in the research and development process. However the effect of competition on innovation is rather controversial, some economists believe that large firms with at least some degree of monopoly power are likely to be most innovative. If this is true, it is not certain that removing the barriers to trade between the members of the EC will improve dynamic efficiency. Indeed it is possible that the static efficiency gains will be more than outweighed by the losses arising from a reduction in dynamic efficiency.

Chapter Five

Externalities 1: external costs

'That's right, Five! Always lay the blame on others!'   Lewis Carroll

What are externalities?

The **external effects** of economic activities are an important reason for markets failing to provide an efficient allocation of resources. **Externalities** happen when costs are imposed on, or when benefits are given to, firms or households who are not parties to the transactions which have these effects. Externalities are by-products or side-effects of production or consumption or both. Examples of **external costs** are found in social, economic and environmental problems such as slum housing, traffic congestion, pollution and the depletion of the ozone layer. **External benefits** arise from public transport, well-maintained housing, education and health care.

If a factory emits pollutants into the air, local households have to spend money on detergents and time on cleaning which would not otherwise be necessary, and some people may become ill because of the polluted atmosphere. These are part of the polluting firm's production costs, but they are imposed on third parties and are not borne by the firm, and they are not charged in the price to the consumers of its products. If public transport makes for less traffic congestion and pollution then car drivers and local inhabitants are the third parties who gain external benefits. However, again, these benefits are external to the market and are not reflected in prices.

The consequences of costs being imposed on others and not included in a product's price leads to **over-production**; the consequence of external benefits not being taken into account in the market is **under-production**. Thus, there is a misallocation of resources to the production of goods which have external effects, and the outcome is not allocatively efficient. Equity, too, is not achieved: costs are imposed on third parties who receive no compensation, and benefits are gained by people who make no payment.

This chapter is about external costs; it shows how over-production comes about and discusses the policies necessary to achieve the optimal level of output and hence an efficient allocation of resources. Chapter 6 is about external benefits, their causes and consequences and how allocative efficiency can be attained where they exist.

External costs

One of the instances in the previous section, air pollution inflicted on neighbouring households by a local firm, is an example of a *producer-to-consumer* externality. A classic example of a *producer-to-producer* external cost is the pollution of river water by an upstream firm when clean water is required by a downstream firm. If the downstream firm has to install equipment to clean the polluted water before it can be used, this is a production cost of the first firm imposed on the second. Alcohol consumption is an activity which causes both *consumer-to-consumer* and *consumer-to-producer* external costs. It causes road accidents and fights which result in hospital bills that are borne by individuals and society; and it impairs workers' efficiency and their health and thereby imposes costs on their employers.

Externalities and the environment

The examples of external costs given so far, though very serious for those who bear them, are all relatively small scale when compared with worldwide environmental problems. **Acid rain**, which crosses national boundaries and arises from sulphur dioxide emissions from coal-fired power stations and nitrogen oxide from vehicles, has long been a problem. More recently concern has grown for the large-scale external costs which can be imposed on the whole planet and on future generations. These are the well-known problems of **global warming** caused by the emission of carbon dioxide (CO_2) and other greenhouse gases and **ozone depletion** by chlorofluorocarbons (CFCs). They are costs of production and consumption

'One, two, three, four, five,
once I caught a fish alive'

45

imposed principally by developed economies on all their own citizens, and on the less developed world, and potentially on future generations.

Global warming may raise sea levels and destroy some of the places where people live and work; it may change climate patterns and reduce food production. Destruction of the ozone layer which protects us from ultraviolet radiation can lead to skin cancers and corneal cataracts. Whether traditional economic analysis and policies based on it are appropriate when the future of the planet may be at stake is a matter of debate and will be discussed in the final section.

External costs: inefficient and unfair

External costs are both inefficient and unfair. Because the producer does not bear all costs and pass them on to the consumer in price, output is extended beyond the allocatively efficient quantity where MSC = MSB. Some units are produced for which social costs exceed social benefits. The inequity arises because third parties have costs imposed on them for which they receive no compensation.

Figure 11 shows how allocative inefficiency arises. There is over-production because the supply curve does not take account of all production costs. The demand curve (D) is the marginal social benefit schedule (MSB) on the assumption that there are no external benefits from consumption. The supply curve (S) is the sum of firms' marginal cost curves, which are **marginal private costs** (MPC) only. However, the production of this good imposes external costs (for example air or water pollution) and these rise as output rises; they are shown by the **marginal external cost** (MXC) curve.

Social costs include both private and external costs. They are shown in the diagram by the **marginal social cost** (MSC) schedule which is obtained when the marginal external cost of each unit is added to the marginal private cost of the unit. The MSC schedule is the vertical sum of MPC and MXC. For example, the unit q' costs society $q's$ (solid arrow), made up of $q't$, the private cost, plus ts, the external cost.

The private market extends production to q_0, where D = S, but for each unit between q^* and q_0 MSC is greater than MSB, these units should not be produced. The **deadweight loss** from their production is the excess of social cost over social benefit for each unit – zero for the unit q^*, up to ac for the unit at q_0, the total amount being given by the triangle abc.

We should note that at q^* external costs will happen – pollution (if this is the cost) is not eliminated; in this example only at output zero are there no external costs. However, for each unit between zero and q^* marginal social benefit is greater than the marginal social cost; that is, benefits are greater than the sum of both private and external costs.

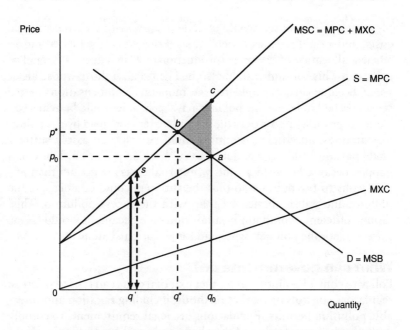

(MXC = marginal external costs; MPC = marginal private costs; MSC = marginal social costs)

Figure 11 External costs and misallocation; output too high and price too low

Therefore it is efficient for each of these units to be produced. The efficient level of pollution, the **optimal externality**, is obtained.

Finally we should note that it is easy to draw a diagram showing external costs precisely, and a precisely quantifiable output which would bring about optimal allocation. In practice, however, estimation of external costs is extremely difficult. Nevertheless a diagrammatic approach is of value because it gives a clear representation of what the problem is.

Property rights and externalities

External costs arise because people have no **property rights** in the good which is used or depleted by those imposing these costs. For example, inhabitants of a neighbourhood do not own the air which surrounds them so they cannot charge the polluting factory for using it as a dump for waste products. The downstream factory does not own the river water and so cannot charge the upstream firm for discharging chemicals into it. If the air and water were owned by these third parties they could charge the polluters for their use of them. This would **internalize the externality,** and all costs would be borne by the producer. The supply curve, private costs, would include what previously were external costs, and would represent social costs. Price would be higher and an efficient allocation of resources (production at q^* in Figure 11) would be achieved. This solution would also be fair because those whose air or water became dirtier would receive monetary compensation for the costs they had to bear. The **'polluter-pays' principle** would be achieved.

Even if property rights over the air and water were held by the polluting factories, an efficient solution could be achieved as the sufferer could pay, or 'bribe', the polluters to cut back on pollution. This could happen because between q^* and q_0 external costs are greater than private gains to the polluter so that the sufferers could compensate the polluter and still be better off than with the excess pollution. This, though efficient, would not be a fair outcome because it would be the sufferers, not the polluter, who paid for pollution abatement.

What can governments do?

Policy to control pollution and other external costs can take two forms: **regulatory controls** or **market methods**, including **taxation** and **tradeable pollution permits**. Regulations are legal requirements to comply with physical standards and they have had some success in the UK in cleaning our air and rivers. Taxation and permits, on the other hand, operate through the price mechanism. In most cases economists prefer market methods as they are more efficient than laws (see box p.50).

Figure 12 shows how taxation can correct the resource misallocation caused by external costs. Like Figure 12 it shows a demand curve (D = MSB) and a supply curve (S = MPC), together with marginal external costs which added to the supply curve give marginal social costs. In addition, tax policy shows how the externality/pollution can be reduced.

A policy to cut output from q_0 to q^* is needed: price must rise. The supply curve needs to be shifted up so that the supply price includes the external cost. The amount by which it needs to be shifted up is the amount of marginal external cost at q^*, which is $q^*e = db$. A unit tax t equal to db shifts the supply curve up to the broken line: supply curve $S + t$. Thus the tax raises price to p^* and cuts output to the allocatively efficient level, q^*. External costs still arise, pollution is not eliminated but it is now an optimal externality. Claiming, as here, that efficiency has been achieved assumes away all the problems of measuring external costs and getting the tax at the right level. In practice these problems are very difficult and very important.

Efficiency is, in theory, achievable; equity, however, is more problematical. Those who benefit from the good whose production or con-

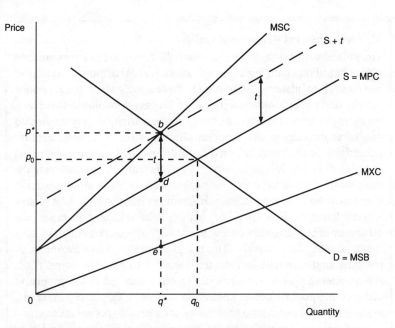

Figure 12 Taxation to reduce an external cost

sumption causes the externality (say pollution) and those who suffer are probably different groups. For example the polluters, who gain benefits, may be car-driving commuters from the suburbs and the sufferers may be those who live near inner-city ring roads and interchanges. The tax paid by the polluters when they buy petrol does not go in compensation to those sufferers, but to the government. If the inner-city dwellers had property rights in the air around them they could have charged commuters for its use. But this solution is possible only in theory; the large numbers which would be involved on both sides of the bargaining process make it unworkable in practice.

Policy for the planet and the future

Finally we should look at the problems listed earlier which may threaten the future of life on earth: global warming and ozone depletion. There are two debates on these problems. The first is in two parts: (a) whether or not they exist, and (b) if they do exist whether they are a matter of concern. The second, assuming that they exist and that something needs to be done, is how to deal with them.

On the first debate there is a minority view that we should not be worried by the environmentalists and their alarmist stories. This opinion is

Environmental economic policy

The groundwork has now been laid for a different kind of environmental policy based on changing *economic incentives*. Traditional 'command and control' regulations can be used to drive a wedge between economic activity and its environmental impact. A flue gas desulphurization plant, for example, leaves the amount of coal-fired electricity largely unaffected but 'takes the sulphur out' from the chimney stack. Economic activity (electricity production) has then been decoupled from environmental impact (acid rain). But there are far more efficient ways of achieving the same thing. The sulphur content of coal could be taxed. The power station then has a choice of how to react. If it reduces sulphur emissions it pays less tax. It may do this by investing in a desulphurization plant, or seeking efficiency improvements, or using lower sulphur coal, or even by switching to another fuel entirely. The tax gives the producer *flexibility* in response and this will lead to the cheapest technology being used. Environmental quality does not suffer, but compared to the command and control approach compliance costs are lower. This is important in a world where environmental regulations daily get tougher not laxer.

An alternative flexible instrument for controlling pollution is the tradeable permit. Instead of taxing the sulphur emissions we could place a 'bubble' over the power generation sector such that the sector as a whole cannot emit more than a certain level of emissions. Within the bubble, however, the industry is free to increase emissions so long as there is an equivalent reduction elsewhere. An efficient procedure is to allow the credits to be traded. We might control vehicle pollution this way as well. Vehicle manufacturers could be given 'miles per gallon' quotas. If they produce cars that do better than the quota, they can sell the resulting credit to other manufacturers. Again, the process is flexible.

The critical features of this economic approach are that it is very likely to cost significantly less than the traditional regulatory approach (US studies suggest savings in compliance costs of at least half); it gives flexibility to polluters; it secures the same environmental quality objectives as the traditional approach; and it stimulates clean technology. After all, the easiest way to avoid environmental taxes or buying permits is to reduce pollution. Gradually, industrialized nations are seeing the virtues of the economic approach. Sweden already has a panoply of environmental taxes; there is CFC tax in the USA and tradeable permits will be widespread under the new acid rain controls.

From: 'Toward the substainable economy: environment and economics' by David Pearce, *Royal Bank of Scotland Review*, Dec. 1991 encapsulated in the writing of Russell Lewis, one-time Director of the Conservative Political Centre. His article in *Economic Affairs*, journal of the right-wing think tank the Institute of Economic Affairs, included the following thoughts:

'• The greens are in retreat
• But two green scares persist
• Even if true a warmer earth might be nicer
• The second ozone hole may only be seasonal
• And if true may not be harmful – ultraviolet rays are decreasing
• Ecology needs the market approach'

However, the majority view among environmental scientists is that it is probable that the problems exist, and that they should be taken very seriously. If we leave it until we are certain before we do anything, then we could be too late.

The last of Lewis's points ('Ecology needs the market approach') takes us on to the second debate. If we assume that there is a fair probability that global warming and ozone depletion exist and that something needs to be done, what form should policy take? For smaller-scale problems it was suggested in the previous section that a market-led approach was more efficient than regulations and laws, and so more likely to result in an optimal outcome. However, the optimal outcome includes the optimal quantity of pollution, the optimal externality. Where the externality may be the destruction of the protective ozone layer, the costs may be unquantifiably large and imposed on future generations, so there may be no optimal quantity of pollution. A market approach, which might permit the continued production of CFCs, would not achieve the desired solution. Regulations, physical controls (for example a ban on CFC production) are needed. 'Inheriting the earth' on p.52, makes the point and links it to the desirable but difficult idea of **sustainable development**.

However, even for the big problems market methods do have a part to play. A favoured method to limit CO_2 emissions is **carbon taxes** which would make the use of fossil fuels and other contributors to greenhouse gases more expensive. This would lead to greater economy in their use, would motivate people to insulate their homes, and would stimulate the development of alternative power sources (for example solar energy) which are at present uneconomic.

External costs vary from the trivial (next-door's bonfire) to the catastrophic (Chernobyl); they affect the present and the future. What this chapter has tried to show is how economic analysis can lead to an understanding of what they are, how they arise, the inefficiency and inequity they cause, and how public policy can deal with them. The aim of policy is to prevent polluters from behaving like Lewis Carroll's Five, always laying the blame on others. However we have found that there may be limits to economic solutions.

Inheriting the earth

No technological fix (not even dark glasses and sun-block) is a satisfactory substitute for a damaged ozone layer. Nor does it make sense to talk of substitutes for extinct species . . . . Moreover, say 'green' economists, to use up unrenewable natural resources, even if we invest the proceeds in man-made capital, is to take a decision on behalf of posterity that our heirs might eventually regret. True fairness to future generations requires that, as far as possible, we leave their options open . . .

Sustainable development is ultimately a frustrating idea. To try to turn it into a usable concept . . . and to apply it to investment decisions or national accounts, exposes some of its weaknesses. It means putting a price on things whose price may be infinite (if, like the ozone layer, they have no substitute) or endlessly debatable (like quietness). It means deciding what value posterity will place on resources that are difficult enough to value today. But as a broad goal, sustainable development is still useful. Like many important ideas, it is better than nothing for as long as there is nothing better.

Source: *The Economist*, 16 Sept. 1989

KEY WORDS

External effects	Marginal social cost
Externalities	Deadweight loss
External costs	Optimal externality
External benefits	Property rights
Over-production	Internalize the externality
Under-production	'Polluter-pays' principle
Acid rain	Regulatory controls
Global warming	Market methods
Ozone depletion	Taxation
Marginal private cost	Tradable pollution permits
Marginal external cost	Sustainable development
	Carbon taxes

Reading list

Anderton, A., *Economics*, Causeway Press, 1991, Unit 35.

Burningham, D., and Davies, J., *Green Economics*, Heinemann Educational, 1994.

Hill, B., 'Green issues', *Journal of the Economics Association*, summer 1991.

Pearce, D., 'Economics and the environment', *Journal of the Economics Association*, spring 1991.

Lewis, R., 'Global hysteria', *Economic Affairs*, vol. 11 (2), 1991.

Essay topics

1. In what sense is the pollution of British rivers and beaches an economic problem? Discuss what economic measures might be taken to deal with pollution in general and explain whether or not you regard it as desirable to try to eliminate it. (Joint Matriculation Board, 1991)

2. Define what is meant by externality. Examine alternative policies to resolve the externality problem in the case of lead pollution from cars. (University of London Examinations and Assessment Council, 1991)

3. Sometimes prices fail to reflect costs fully. In the light of this statement, how would an economist deal with problems such as pollution and traffic congestion? (University of Cambridge Local Examinations Syndicate, 1990)

4. 'As with all externalities, the proper way to treat them is to make those who cause environmental damage pay for it.' Discuss. (Oxford and Cambridge Schools Examination Board, 1990)

Data Response Question 5

'How can the recent tradition of tax reform be continued? One answer: explore environmental taxes. Most taxes raise revenue, but do economic harm – by penalising jobs, say, or profits. Green taxes can raise money and do good, by making polluters pay costs they otherwise pass on to others. That is more efficient than allowing polluters to treat air, water and lovely views as though they were free. Taxes are also often more efficient than regulation.

The simplest green tax would be on road transport. Plenty of transport taxes already exist, so no new tax need be dreamt up; lots of costs – congestion, lead and many nasty gases - are inflicted by motorists on others; and road traffic will be a growing source of pollution. The transport department projects a doubling in the number of miles travelled by 2025. So even to restrict pollution to present levels would mean halving emissions per mile. On present trends, the reverse may happen: the 20% rise in new car registrations between 1983 and 1988 has been entirely due to a rise in the number of cars with engines over 1500cc. Bigger cars usually use more fuel.

There are various ways of applying green taxes to transport including using taxes to reduce fuel consumption.

One way would be to raise petrol duty. High petrol prices give motorists an incentive to drive fewer miles, and to increase their miles per gallon. The real price of petrol is low by historic standards. To raise prices to their peak of 1975 would need an increase in duty from 93p a gallon on 4-star to about 148p. Impossible? Britain's petrol duty would still be lower than Italy's.

The Institute of Fiscal Studies calculates that a 55p rise in duty would cut petrol consumption by nearly 8% (more in the longer run, as people bought smaller cars). It would raise £1.8 billion in revenue directly, and indirectly another £300m. If changes in the commercial use of petrol mirrored those in the personal sector, revenue might be another £900m higher – a total of at least £3 billion.

Most of the tax increase would fall on middle-income and wealthy households – the poorest rarely own cars. But among car-owners, the poorest tenth would find a 55p rise in duty took 2% of their gross incomes; the richest tenth would lose less than 0.7%.

Other EC countries have higher car taxes on big cars. That would encourage people to buy smaller cars. But would it cut fuel consumption? Not necessarily. Car duty has no effect on the cost of an extra mile driven. And, while most small cars use less fuel per mile than big ones, some don't.

(Source: adapted from an article in *The Economist journal*, *The Economist Newspaper*, 27 January 1990, which referred to an Institute of Fiscal Studies *Commentary*, No. 19.)

1. Suggest *two* reasons why the real price of petrol has fallen since 1975.
2. Analyse the effects of a 55p rise in petrol duty on (i) government finances and (ii) income distribution.
3. Compare the effectiveness of using increased petrol duty and differential rates of vehicle excise duty ('car tax') as methods of cutting fuel consumption.
4. Using a diagram, explain how environmental taxes can be used to help reduce the problem of pollution.

(University of London Examinations and Assessment Council, 1993)

Chapter Six
Externalities 2: external benefits

'A cat may look at a king', said Alice.   Lewis Carroll

External benefits
Externalities were defined in the previous chapter where external costs were analysed. Here we turn to **external benefits**, their causes and consequences and how allocative efficiency can be attained where they exist. Much of the discussion turns on the provision of **public goods** and **mixed goods**. Where externalities cannot explain public provision we turn to distribution and equity arguments.

External benefits, like external costs, are by-products of production and consumption; they are positive side-effects which raise welfare. As with external costs, there may be producer-to-producer effects (for example skills training which workers take with them when they move); producer-to-consumer effects; and consumer-to-consumer effects (for example a well-maintained house enhances the value of the house next door). Many external benefits, from services like public transport, education or refuse collection, come from simultaneous consumption and production. The extract in the box entitled 'The Harrogate Conference Centre: they meant well' on p. 56 illustrates external benefits. You might consider the questions posed in the last few lines of the extract.

Goods that provide external benefits are known as mixed goods and are under-provided by the market. Mixed goods are a sub-category of public goods, the main category being pure public goods. These are goods which in effect are all externality because none of their benefits can be confined to those prepared to pay. The best known example is national defence. The precise attributes which make goods public goods are discussed later in this chapter.

External benefits and misallocation
Where there were external costs we found that there was over-provision; conversely, where there are external benefits, there is under-provision. There is **allocative inefficiency** because the market fails to provide some units of the good or service for which social benefits exceed social costs. Figure 13, on the next page, shows how this happens.

The Harrogate Conference Centre: they meant well

Since its days as a spa, Harrogate has lived off visitors. In the 1970s it seemed commonsense to complement its existing exhibition halls with an up-to-date centre for the booming conference business.

The original, mid-1970s estimate was just under £8m. The final cost, agreed only this month, after six years of operation, was £34m: a worse-than-Concorde burden for its owner, a modest district council.

If only Harrogate were Labour-run Islington, free-marketeers in Brighton this week (at the Conservative Party conference) would have had yet another wondrous case of town-hall lunacy to make fun of. But it is not: Harrogate has been Conservative-run throughout. And for all the errors of execution, local Tories still argue that the intention was sound. The conference centre was built, and is run even now, quite specifically, to benefit the local economy as a whole, not just to show a bottom-line profit for its owners. The centre and its halls are well filled, by industry standards; consultants suggest that they bring £50m–60m a year into the area. Their future may well lie in private ownership or at least management. But would the centre ever have got off the ground if the council had not built it? If not, ought it to have remained unbuilt? The answers are not as self-evident in Harrogate as in Brighton.

Source: *The Economist*, 15 Oct. 1988

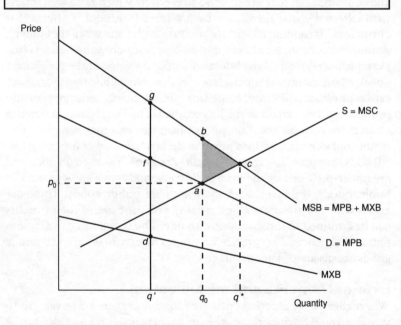

(MSC = marginal social costs; MXB = marginal external benefits; MPB = marginal private benefit)

Figure 13 External benefits and misallocation

In Figure 13, assuming that there are no external costs, private and social costs are the same: the supply curve, marginal private costs, also represents marginal social costs. The market demand curve is the sum of all consumers' marginal benefit (utility) curves which are marginal private benefits (MPB) only. However, the production and consumption of the good or service, say public transport, gives benefits (emptier roads and less pollution) to other road users and people who live near traffic routes. These are external benefits and do not enter the private demand schedule. They are shown by the marginal external benefit schedule (MXB). Marginal external benefits are *estimated* because demand for external benefits is not known (see on to 'public goods' for why this is so).

Social benefits include all benefits, private and external, and are shown in the diagram as the marginal social benefit schedule (MSB). For each unit MSB is obtained by adding together private and external benefits: for unit q' private benefits are $q'f$, external benefits are $q'd$, and social benefits are $q'g$ which is external benefits ($fg = q'd$) added to private benefits. Thus the marginal social benefit (MSB) curve is marginal external benefits (MXB) added vertically to marginal private benefits (MPB).

The private market leads to production at q_0, where the supply and demand curves intersect; but at q_0 and beyond there are units which add more to social benefits than to social cost. For maximum welfare (**allocative efficiency**) every unit up to q^* should be produced. The **deadweight loss** which arises from the market's failure to take account of external benefits is shown by the excess of social benefit over social cost for each unit between q_0 and q^* and is the shaded area *abc*.

Public goods
Public goods are part of a spectrum which ranges from pure public goods to pure private goods, with mixed goods in between. There is no market demand curve for a public good; this, and the consequent allocative inefficiency, comes about because of the special characteristics of public goods. For a private good consumption is rival – my eating an apple prevents your eating it; and exclusion from benefit of those not prepared to pay is feasible – if you will not pay for the apple the seller will keep it (i.e. will exclude you). However, a public good is not like an apple:

- *either* consumption is non-rival
- *or* exclusion is not feasible
- *or* both of these characteristics are present.

First, consider **non-rival consumption**. This means that an additional consumer adds nothing to cost. For example, an additional pedestrian on a well-lit street does not add to the cost of lampposts, lights and electricity; or an additional car crossing an uncrowded bridge adds nothing to cost. (It would be different if the bridge were crowded, when it would add to congestion which imposes time and fuel costs.) Being able to see the road at night, or being able to cross a river adds to consumer welfare without adding anything to cost.

For allocative efficiency, that is to maximize welfare, every consumer who wishes to use the bridge (up to the point where it becomes congested) should be able to do so. A toll, though feasible, would be inefficient since it would reduce welfare by preventing some people from using the bridge, without any matching cost reduction. If the toll charge were £1, everyone who valued crossing at less than that amount would not cross, and would be deprived of 95 pence-worth or 60 pence-worth, and so on, of benefit. For maximum welfare goods with a marginal cost of consumption of zero ($MC = 0$) should have a price equal to zero ($p = MC$). No private firm would undertake the production of a good for which price is zero. A private bridge owner would charge a toll which would be allocatively inefficient because it would deter potential beneficiaries without saving any costs. (It must be noted that it is the **marginal cost of consumption** which is zero; the **marginal cost of production** of these goods is not zero: the cost of an additional *consumer* of street lighting is zero, but the cost of an additional *street light* is positive.)

The second characteristic of a public good is **non-exclusion**. Non-exclusion means that it is not feasible to exclude non-payers from benefit. Here it is not the case, as with the bridge, that market provision is undesirable; it is that market provision is impossible. Take national defence or clean streets as examples: most people want their country to be defended and to walk in litter-free streets. However, if these services are provided then even those not prepared to pay benefit. An individual will reason: 'Why should I pay if my neighbour who refuses to pay benefits equally? I won't pay.' If everyone wants to be a **free-rider** like this – and where numbers are large this is what happens – then preferences are not revealed and the service is not provided.

As well as national defence, street lights and empty bridges, public goods also include law and order (provided by the combined services of police, law courts and prisons), flood protection, roads, national parks, and medical and other research. For some of them consumption is non-rival and exclusion is not feasible (for example street lights, and national parks when uncongested); for others, though, exclusion is feasible, consumption is non-rival (for example an uncongested motorway); for others consumption is rival but exclusion is not feasible (for example busy city roads, though electronic road pricing will change this).

Externalities are non-rival and non-excludable. A public good is, in effect, all externality, and so there is no private demand schedule. This does not mean, however, as is sometimes argued, that there is 'joint' demand for public goods. People do not jointly or collectively demand street lights or law and order: as with any good, *individuals* have preferences for them (they are in individuals' preference functions). A nuclear disarmer's preferences for defence would be very different from those of a person who wanted 'strong defences'. Society's demand for defence is the sum of many different individual preferences; this is the case for all public goods.

Finally, it should be made clear that public goods are goods for which the market fails, either completely or in part. Public sector ownership of plant and equipment, and organization of production, does not make the output a public good. For example, postal services and coal (and before privatization, electricity, gas, telecommunications and so on) are produced within the public sector, but they are private goods.

Mixed goods

Mixed goods, as the name suggests, provide a mixture of private and external benefits. *Like private goods they are rival in consumption and are excludable.* (If I am in a hospital bed receiving treatment you cannot use it, so an extra patient adds to cost; and if you cannot provide evidence of your ability to pay you could be refused treatment.) Therefore preferences are revealed and the market works. However, *mixed goods also give non-rival, non-excludable external benefits for which preferences are not revealed.* Only private benefits are reflected in market demand and, as the first section of this chapter showed, the market under-provides.

Health care, education, public transport, refuse collection and the fire service are all mixed goods. The balance of private benefit and external benefit varies between them. For health care it seems likely that the balance is fairly heavily weighted towards private benefits, with the person who receives treatment gaining more than the community; but there are protective side-effects (against infectious disease) and productive side-effects (getting workers back to work). Some claim that education, too, provides only small external benefits, but others take an opposing view, arguing that a well-educated workforce raises productivity, exports and economic growth, which benefits everyone in an economy.

For public transport the balance between private, internal, benefits and external benefits moves towards a fairly large proportion of external benefits, particularly in large cities where a good public system keeps the whole city moving. Every individual and business in the city benefits, whether they use public transport or not. Similarly a good national rail network benefits business, road users and the whole economy. The Director General of the British Institute of Management recently remarked: 'Continued emphasis on the primacy of private transport will eventually work against the interest of the majority of users – and of the efficiency of the UK as a whole'.

Finally, the fire service is an example of a mixed good where external benefits are likely to outweigh internal. If firefighters put out a blaze in a chemical factory they benefit not only the chemical firm but also a large surrounding area which they save from explosions and pollution. If they put out a fire in a single flat they may save from fire every apartment in the same building.

The role for government

Pure public goods
Where the market fails completely the public sector must provide. For efficiency it should provide in line with people's preferences, which is where demand (MSB) and supply (we assume, MSC) curves intersect. However, though there could be market supply schedules for street lights, defence goods, flood protection and so on, there is no possibility of market demand schedules for them. This is not because individual demand does not exist but because it is not revealed. If people could be persuaded to reveal their preferences, to show what they would pay for different quantities of each public good, then a market demand schedule could be constructed. Market demand could interact with market supply and an efficient level of output could be arrived at.

However, such demand schedules do not exist. In **democracies** governments determine public provision. At election times people vote for the party whose public spending (and tax) plans are most in line with their preferences. Whether or not the outcome is that public goods are provided in line with **majority preferences** is a matter of debate. Some economists have argued that biases in the democratic process lead to under-provision, a smaller quantity of public goods than people really want. For example, Pigou thought that people would take account only of internal benefits when voting; and Galbraith ('private affluence and public squalor') thought that people would favour private goods, which are associated with the merits of the market, over public goods, damned by association with the state. Others, the New Right, argue that there are biases which lead to over-provision and more public expenditure than people really want. They think that this happens because the benefits are obvious to voters but that the costs are not: voters think that others will pay the taxes which buy public goods. The outcome of the last four elections in the UK appears to contradict this.

Once the overall size of the public budget and each spending programme has been decided, then **cost-benefit analysis** may be used to determine whether a particular project should be undertaken or to choose between alternative projects. *CBA is an efficiency technique which assesses both costs and benefits; it takes into account external as well as internal effects and looks ahead into the future:* CBA takes 'a wide view and a long view'. However, CBA may be used to support a project which has already been selected on political grounds; for example a particular route for a new road.

Mixed goods

Here the government's function is again to try to provide the optimum quantity in line with external as well as private demand. This is shown in Figure 14 on p.62. The market quantity is q_0 at price p_0. The efficient, welfare maximizing, quantity is q^*, which would happen if price to the buyer were lower at p_b, and price to the seller were higher, at p_s. To achieve this a subsidy is necessary, of size s, the difference between supply price and demand price at q^*. The new demand curve, including the subsidy, is the broken line D_sD_s. Again the qualification must be made: it is easy to draw a schedule showing external effects and to show the optimum quantity of output. In practice external benefits are very difficult to quantify and to put a value on.

(We should note that in drawing a marginal external benefit (MXB) curve, both here and in Figure 13, we have assumed away the difficulties noted earlier about the revelation of preferences for benefits which are non-excludable. The MXB curve is the external beneficiaries pseudo-demand curve for, say, public transport. This pseudo-demand curve cannot be known, but in the case of public transport some quantification of external benefits, value of time saved, fuel saved and so on, is possible.)

Figure 14 could represent the demand and supply curves for bus services in a city, together with an estimate of the external benefits of those services and of the size of subsidy required. For other mixed goods (in particular education, but also health care in many countries) rather than subsidy there is free public provision paid for by taxation. In this case, for efficiency, the government should aim to provide the welfare maximizing quantity in line with private and external preferences.

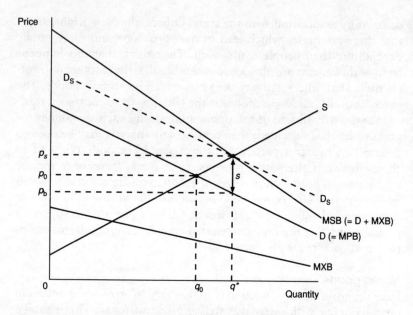

The market provides quantity q_0 at price p_0. The welfare maximising quantity is q^*. A subsidy of size s would shift the demand curve up to D_s and raise the equilibrium quantity to q^*. Sellers would receive price p_s, buyers would pay only p_b

Figure 14 External benefits and public subsidy

Equity and merit goods

The New Right dispute much of the argument on mixed goods and claim that the external benefits from education and health care, in particular, are very small, and no justification for public provision. Some economists who are not on the political right tend to agree that these services' external benefits are not large, so that they cannot be used to justify state provision. However, this does not lead them to conclude, as do the New Right, that health care and education should be left to the market. They argue that individual preferences about the kind of society we want to live in provide the justification for public provision. If the majority want children to be educated and access to health care to depend on need rather than on the ability to pay for it, then a democratic society will provide this. *This argument is based on equity not on efficiency.*

Finally something needs to be said about what are termed '**merit goods**'. These are goods which are so 'meritorious' that the government overrides consumer preferences and provides the quantity which it thinks people ought to consume. Health care and education, which are mixed goods, may also be classified as merit goods. There are no efficiency arguments here, no economic analysis underlies the concept of merit goods. We should think of them as **redistribution in kind**. It is argued that taxpayers are more prepared to provide free education and health care than cash benefits. Though some goods fall into both the mixed and the merit goods categories there is a clear distinction between the two and the terms should not be used interchangeably. In the case of mixed goods the function of the public sector is to provide the efficient quantity, in line with (internal and external) consumers' preferences. In the case of merit goods there are no efficiency arguments, and consumers' preferences may be overruled.

KEY WORDS

External benefits	Marginal cost of production
Public goods	Non-exclusion
Mixed goods	Free-rider
Allocative inefficiency	Democracies
Allocative efficiency	Majority preferences
Deadweight loss	Cost-benefit analysis
Non-rival consumption	Merit goods
Marginal cost of consumption	Redistribution in kind

Reading list

Anderton, A., *Economics*, Causeway Press, 1991, Units 36 and 44.

Beardshaw, J., Chapter 2 in *Economics: A Student's Guide*, 3rd edn, Pitman, 1992.

Whynes, D., Chapter 2 in *Welfare State Economics*, Heinemann Educational, 1992.

Essay topics

1. Distinguish between 'merit goods' and 'demerit goods'. How, and to what extent, should the government provide merit goods and discourage the provision of demerit goods? (Joint Matriculation Board, A/S level, 1991)

2. What problems exist in deciding how much should be spent on the provision of public and merit goods? (Oxford and Cambridge Schools Examination Board, 1991)

3. Define and give examples of external costs and external benefits. Explain and comment on the policies which a government may

adopt to reduce external costs and increase external benefits. (University of Cambridge Local Examinations Syndicate, 1991)
4. Briefly examine the following terms: (i) externalities, (ii) cost-benefit analysis. The government is proposing to build a motorway linking a city with a major port. This motorway would cross an area of outstanding natural beauty. Discuss the problems involved in undertaking a cost-benefit analysis of such a project. (University of London Examinations and Assessment Council, 1992)
5. (a) Distinguish between a 'public good', a 'merit good' and a 'private good'. (b) Using defence and education as examples, examine the economic arguments used to justify the provision of public goods and merit goods. (University of London Examinations and Assessment Council 1992).

Data Response Question 6

Vision versus profits
Read the newspaper leading article on the page opposite and answer the questions.

1. Summarize the leader writer's main argument.
2. Support the argument with economic analysis – using concepts such as externalities and social optimum output.
3. How would you start on a cost-benefit analysis of BR investment in a railway from London to the Channel Tunnel, together with new rail links across London?

Listen to Sir Robert

The battle for industrial survival in the barrier-free Europe of the mid-1990s may well be won or lost by the quality of infrastructure. But it may already have been lost for Britain. While France and Germany have been laying imaginative foundations for motorways, cross-city rail links and a continent-wide network of high-speed trains, Britain has made a virtue of containing public spending and removing subsidies from BR. The statistics were laid out starkly by a report by a House of Lords committee showing that investment in road infrastructure between 1982 and 1985 as a percentage of gross domestic product was 0.8 per cent in West Germany, 0.65 per cent in France – and just 0.40 per cent in Britain. Spending on railways was even worse – only 0.09 per cent in Britain, compared with 0.26 per cent in Italy and 0.29 per cent in Belgium. We made the profits while they built the railways.

The emerging map of new high-speed rail links planned or built across Europe is an impressive spaghetti of interlocking routes from the South of Spain to the North of France where it grinds to a halt at Calais. A small dotted line from Dover to London is Britain's contribution – if ever we get round to raising enough money privately. It is in this context that this week's valedictory speech by Sir Robert Reid, the retiring chairman of British Rail, is so important. Here is a man who has done extremely well in delivering the government's brief. Subsidies are gradually being removed, fares hiked, productivity impressively improved and investment increased from internally generated funds. Much of this may have been obscured from the long-suffering commuter by the explosive growth of passenger journeys, but the achievement is real. But also, as Sir Robert now admits publicly, having failed to convince the government privately, it was not the brief which should have been addressed. It was a journey without maps.

Sir Robert urged the speedy construction of a railway from London to the Channel Tunnel, new rail links across London and, most important, suggested that "in certain circumstances" BR's new investment should be judged on the basis of cost-benefit analysis. This means that instead of judging new lines solely on whether they would be profitable to BR, criteria like reduction of accidents and road congestion should be taken into account. If the criteria the government has forced on BR were applied to high-speed railways on the continent, it is quite possible none of them would be built. But they know over there the incalculable advantage of a high-speed transport infrastructure in attracting international investment and lowering industry's costs when the real battle for Europe commences. Lyon has been galvanised by its fast link running from Paris down to the Mediterranean. Where is the vision in Britain?

Source: *The Guardian*, 10 Jan. 1990

Chapter Seven
Taxes

'The rule is, jam tomorrow and jam yesterday – but never jam today.'   Lewis Carroll

Taxes are '*compulsory, unrequited* payments to general government' (OECD). They affect income distribution (equity) and economic performance (efficiency). Around the world in the 1980s, **tax reform** was near the top of the political agenda. 'Tax reform' is shorthand for making the tax system more efficient, less distortionary. It may be characterized as 'set the lowest possible rate on the widest possible base' – that is, for any tax there should be a low rate with the fewest possible reliefs. If the tax rate is low then people have less incentive to change their behaviour to avoid tax; and if reliefs and exemptions are few this removes the distortions which happen when people and companies attempt to make the sources and uses of their income fit tax-exempt categories. However, changes to taxes affect income distribution as well as economic performance and in tax policy the principles of efficiency and equity frequently conflict. For example, a tax on income may distort the choice between work and leisure but such a tax may be desirable on the grounds of fairness.

Taxes and efficiency
People do not like paying taxes. In order to avoid them (which is legal: *evasion* is the illegal non-payment of tax due) they change their behaviour. For example they work less and earn less and so pay less income tax; or they buy goods which are not taxed rather than taxed goods (not deliberately, but untaxed goods have relatively lower prices); or they save and invest by putting their money in houses rather than by buying shares in industry, because paying mortgage interest frees some income from tax.

   This **distortion of choice** reduces welfare. There is clearly a minimum amount by which paying tax must reduce welfare; this is the resource transfer which the tax represents. It is known as the **minimum burden** of taxation. But taxes frequently reduce welfare by more than this and then there is an **excess burden**. The aim of efficiency is to minimize distortions to keep the excess burden as low as possible. There will always be some excess; it cannot be eliminated entirely because the actions which would reduce it would make the system less fair, and there have to be trade-offs between objectives. A fairly trivial example of inefficiency is given in the box headed 'The window tax'.

The window tax

The window tax of 1695 was based on the number of windows a taxpayer owned. Rich people had big houses and many windows and the less well-off had smaller houses and fewer windows, and so it seems a fair tax. The revenue raised represented the transfer of resources from the people to their rulers and this welfare reduction was the minimum burden of the tax. However, it had other effects which further reduced welfare. People who wanted to cut their tax liability had windows bricked up and new houses were built with fewer windows. Bricked-up windows and darker rooms reduced welfare but raised no revenue. This welfare loss over and above the minimum represented by the tax payment was the excess burden of the window tax.

Income tax

There are many present-day examples of the way taxes distort behaviour. Both **income tax** and expenditure taxes impose excess burdens. The excess burden of income tax arises because choice between work and leisure is distorted. When a tax is imposed income from work falls, and so does the **opportunity cost of leisure**. For example, if the wage rate is £10 per hour, then one hour's leisure costs £10 (foregone); if a 30 per cent tax has to be paid the price of leisure falls to £7 per hour. People will take more leisure and work less when they have to pay income tax. There is a **substitution effect**: workers substitute leisure for work. It is this reasoning which gives rise to the argument that taxes are **disincentives** to work.

However, as well as the substitution effect which reduces work effort, there is also an **income effect** which increases it. Paying taxes (in effect, lower wage rates) means that people have less income and can afford less of all normal goods, including leisure, and so they work longer hours. Another way of putting this is that if a worker needs a certain income to pay for housing, food, clothes and so on then, when tax has to be paid, more hours must be worked to achieve it.

Figures 15 and 16, individual labour supply schedules (which assumes that individuals are free to vary their hours of work), show the combined results of the two effects.

In Figure 16 the reduction in the wage rate from W_1 to W_0, caused by income tax, results in the number of hours at work falling from L_1 to L_0. For this worker the substitution effect outweighs the income effect and the tax is a disincentive.

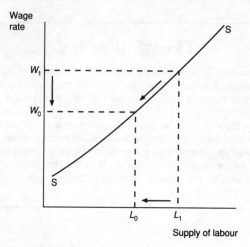

Figure 15 Normal labour supply curve

In Figure 16, however, the opposite is the case: the tax-induced fall in the wage rate results in more hours being worked (L_1 to L_0. For this individual the income effect is the stronger, and the labour supply curve bends backwards.

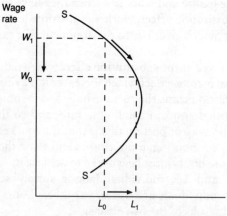

Figure 16 Backward bending labour supply curve

Income tax cuts in the 1980s to give **incentives** to workers and employers to boost the **supply side** of the economy were based on the assumption that labour supply curves were as shown in Figure 15 with the substitution effect the stronger. Empirical work shows that for most workers this is not the case.

Expenditure tax

Expenditure taxes, too, impose excess burdens. This is illustrated in Figure 17. SS is the supply curve before tax and DD the demand curve; equilibrium is at e_1, with price op_1 and quantity oq_1. When a unit tax is imposed the supply curve shifts up by the amount of the tax, t, to S_tS_t. (A unit tax is a given amount per unit of the product: for example excise duty of £5.75 per bottle of whisky or 38 pence per pint on beer (1990–91).) The supply curve shift shows that sellers add the full amount of the tax to the supply price. Consumers resist: they change their behaviour and buy less of the good. A new equilibrium is attained at e_2, with a higher price to the consumer op_2 and a lower quantity, oq_2. The price received by the seller is og, sale price less unit tax. The total revenue raised is the quantity sold (oq_2) multiplied by the tax per unit ($t = ae_2$) = gp_2e_2a.

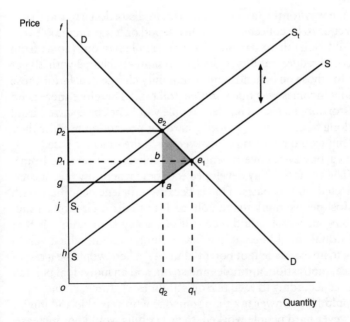

Figure 17 The excess burden of a unit tax on sales

The loss of welfare for consumers and producers is greater than the total revenue raised. Before the tax was imposed the **consumers' surplus** (the area under the demand curve and above the price line) was p_1fe_1, after tax it is p_2fe_2, so the loss of consumers' surplus is $p_1p_2e_2e_1$. Before tax the **producers' surplus** (the area above the supply curve and below the price line) was p_1e_1h, after tax it is gah, so the loss of **producers' surplus** is p_1e_1ag. When consumers' and producers' lost surpluses are added together we find that the total welfare loss is the heavily bordered area $gp_2e_2e_1a$. This loss is greater than the transfer of resources to the government (society) via taxation (gp_2e_2a). The excess burden or **deadweight loss** is represented by the difference between the two areas, the shaded triangle ae_2e_1.

There is, however, a circumstance when a sales tax may *increase* efficiency: this is in the case when a good imposes external costs, of production or of consumption. In this case the supply curve does not represent social costs and a rise in price and reduction in quantity is efficient. For example, a unit tax on alcohol, which causes road accidents and poor performance at work, raises the price and cuts consumption, which is efficient (see Figure 12 in Chapter 5).

A poll tax

There is one way for the tax system to be non-distortionary, and that is for all revenue to be collected from a **head, poll or lump-sum tax**. Every adult would be liable to pay and no change in behaviour (apart from suicide) could reduce liability. (The UK community charge with 20 per cent bills for those on benefits, and community charge benefit for those on very low incomes was not a *simple* poll tax.) Therefore there is no choice distortion, no excess burden. People would not be deterred from working long hours or from working hard for promotion because their fixed tax bill would not change however much their income rose.

In practice, however, governments do not collect their revenue from a poll tax. The UK is the only developed economy where any revenue has been collected on this basis. This is because efficiency conflicts with equity. Most people think that a poll tax is not fair. A far-fetched suggestion, but one which could reconcile efficiency with equity, is that each individual should be liable to pay a lump sum tax which varied according to an assessment of potential to pay. There would be a test of intelligence, motivation, aptitudes and so on, and an individual poll tax would be set according to each person's abilities. A stupid, clumsy individual would face a lower tax than someone who was able and intelligent. However hard people worked, their tax bills would not increase. But though the idea is interesting it is not remotely likely that such a tax would be introduced; apart from other problems the practical difficulties would be insurmountable.

Equity

Equity involves value judgements, and judgements on whether something is fair vary between people. For example, supporters of the poll tax argued that it was fair because it required people who used local services to pay for them. This represents the **benefit approach** to equity. Those who thought it unfair did so because it took no account of income – they applied the **ability-to-pay approach**. It was not merely those on the political left and centre who criticized the poll tax, many Conservatives also thought it unfair.

The benefit approach to equity is mainly of historical interest. Modern governments of all political persuasions use ability to pay to judge the fairness of taxes. This, however, does not mean that there is no room for differences of view on precisely how the principle should be applied.

Alternative tax patterns

A is a low earner on £8000 per year, B has a comfortable income of £20000, and C is a high earner on £40000 a year. The tax bills each face for all taxes paid, direct plus indirect plus taxes shifted by companies, could be very different, even if the tax bill rises as income rises. For example, three possible patterns of tax payment on the lowest to the highest income, respectively, could be:

(reading across: row (1), then row (2), then row (3))

		Taxpayer A (£8000)	Taxpayer B (£20 000)	Taxpayer C (£40 000)
Either	(1)	£2400	£6000	£12 000
or	(2)	£1200	£5000	£14 000
or	(3)	£2400	£5000	£8000

In each of these alternatives the lowest income pays the least absolute amount of tax, and the highest pays the most. If this is an interpretation of the ability to pay, each alternative accords with the principle. However the patterns of tax are very different. Under alternative (1) taxes are **proportional** to income, taking 30 per cent from each taxpayer. Alternative (2) represents **a progressive** system: the proportion of income taken in tax rises from 15 per cent on the lowest, to 25 per cent in the middle to 35 per cent on the highest income. Alternative (3) shows **regressive** taxation; though the lowest income pays absolutely least and the highest absolutely most, the proportion of income taken in tax falls as income rises: from 30 per cent (on £8000), to 25 per cent, to 20 per cent (on £40 000).

Taxes on expenditure tend to be regressive, taxes on income, progressive. The balance between indirect and direct taxation can determine whether the whole system tends towards progression or regression.

Economists have no more right than any other citizens to say what the fair treatment of people with unequal incomes, and unequal ability to pay, should be. However, they can help clarify the issues and the concept of **equal sacrifice** was devised for this purpose. Equal sacrifice means that paying taxes should involve every taxpayer in an equal sacrifice of utility or welfare. If the marginal utility of income falls as income rises, this means that paying £1 in tax is a greater sacrifice for a poor person than for a rich one, which suggests that the rich should pay more pounds than the poor in order to sacrifice the same utility. This, however, is only the start of the arguments based on equal sacrifice.

Agreeing that it is fair that the rich should pay more than the poor does not get us very far, as the examples in the box headed 'Alternative tax patterns' shows. It demonstrates that agreement on the ability-to-pay principle leaves a large area for disagreement on the distribution of the burden.

There is much more to be said on this. Getting the right pattern of taxes on unequal incomes raises questions of both efficiency (disincentive effects of high taxes) and equity which will be pursued further in the final chapter on poverty.

British taxes

The British tax system is very far from perfect. In this section we assess the view that changes to British taxes in the 1980s increased efficiency but at the expense of equity.

Mrs Thatcher liked to think of herself as a tax reformer, improving the supply side of the economy by giving incentives to employers and workers. In one case (corporation tax) reform was undertaken in textbook fashion: in 1984 the rate was reduced from 52 to 35 per cent and the base was widened by the reduction of tax-free investment allowances. However, for other taxes the picture is less clear. For the two large revenue raisers, personal income tax and value added tax, big changes were made but the analysis which follows shows that it is unlikely that there were large efficiency gains. And the slight tax progression (over all attributable taxes) of the 1970s disappeared; over a wide range of incomes the system became regressive.

Starting with their first budget in 1979 and finishing in the 1987 budget, Conservative governments reduced the basic rate of income tax from 33 to 25 per cent, and the top rate from 83 to 40 per cent. Figure 18 on p.74 shows how large the changes were. At the same time, to compensate for revenue lost from income tax, the VAT rate was increased from 8 to 15 per cent. The effects of these changes were to reduce the proportion of revenue from income tax and to increase the proportion from VAT. In 1978 income tax raised 35 per cent and VAT 10 per cent of total revenue; by 1990 the income tax contribution had fallen to 27 per cent and the VAT contribution had risen to 17 per cent (calculated from *National Accounts (Bluebook)* estimates). Income tax is progressive, expenditure taxes are regressive, and by 1990 over a wide range of incomes the total tax burden was regressive.

Table 1 shows the effects on households ranked by income of all attributable taxes – direct, indirect and intermediate (those paid by companies, for example employers' National Insurance contributions, but assumed to be shifted on to consumers in product prices). Row 1 excludes gross rates, the inclusion of which would have distorted the estimate for the bottom quintile (who paid much lower net rates), so that tax burdens across the whole income range can be compared. For the bottom two quintiles (fifths), excluding rates, the system is progressive. However, if all attributable taxes, including rates, are considered (row 2), then in 1988, excluding the bottom quintile, the tax system was regressive. Households in the top quintile paid a smaller proportion of gross income in taxes than did households in the quintile next to the bottom; and moving from the third, to the fourth, to the top quintile of incomes, tax proportions fell.

If tax in proportion to income or tax progression is regarded as fair, then fairness was reduced in the 1980s. From being progressive at the

Table 1 Taxes as a percentage of household income by quintile income groups, 1988

| | Quintile groups* | | | | |
	Bottom fifth	Next fifth	Middle fifth	Next fifth	Top fifth
Average income per household	3571	6781	11 576	17 149	32 307
Direct and indirect taxes including 'intermediate' taxes† as percentage of gross income:					
(1) excluding gross rates	25.3	30.7	34.6	35.4	32.8
(2) including gross rates	‡	37.8	39.9	38.7	35.0

* Ranked by disposable income.
† Producers' taxes (employers' National Insurance contributions, rates, petrol duty, etc.) passed on to consumers in product prices.
‡ The use of data for gross rates would provide a considerable overestimate for this quintile. For the other quintiles it is assumed that gross and net rates coincide.
Source: 'The effects of taxes and benefits on household income, 1988'. Table 1, Appendix 3, *Economic Trends*, January 1991

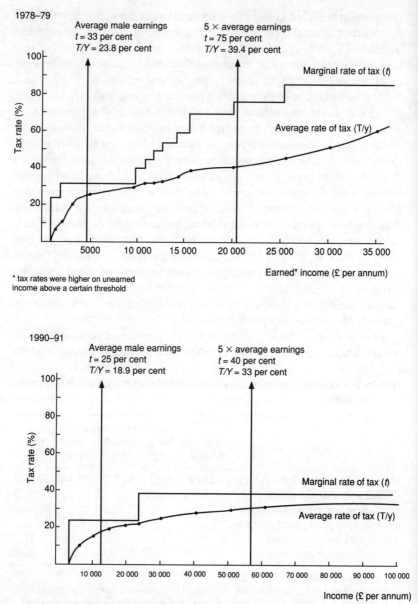

Figure 18 Marginal and average rates of income tax for a single person

bottom of the income range to proportional at the top (1978 data in *Economic Trends*, 1980), taxes became regressive over a wide range of incomes, though progression or proportionality was achieved at the bottom. This outcome was the cumulative effect of changes to income tax, VAT and National Insurance contributions. Corporation tax and poll tax, which have opposing effects to each other on progression, are not included in these results.

Income tax cuts, which reduced progression, were intended to make the system more efficient, to boost the supply side. However, though lower income tax rates make people substitute work for leisure, there is the offsetting income effect which makes for less work. In addition income tax cuts were made possible by VAT increases, and tax on workers' expenditures has the same consequence as tax on their incomes: 'direct' taxes reduce money income, 'indirect' taxes raise prices, and in either case real income is reduced. Economists argue that it makes no difference to workers' incentives where, in the getting and spending of their incomes, they are taxed; only in the short-run might they be 'misled into working harder' by a transfer from direct to indirect taxation. Rational, maximizing economic agents are under no money illusion and therefore the income tax cuts for basic rate taxpayers (the large majority), paid for by VAT increases, should not be expected to have large effects on incentives. There could be some effect if some income is saved, and some spent on goods not liable to VAT; for example housing. And voting behaviour would indicate that, at least for some, money illusion exists, because even basic rate income taxpayers appear to believe that Conservative governments in the 1980s cut tax burdens. For those paying at rates above the basic rate the larger cuts in the higher marginal rates would more than compensate for VAT increases and, as long as income effects did not completely offset them, lower taxes would have had the incentive effects intended. The verdict on Conservative tax policy under Mrs Thatcher may be summarized as a little more efficient but a lot less fair. In the 1980s, for those with high incomes, the epigraph which started the chapter is wrong: they got more 'jam today'.

> ### KEY WORDS
>
> | | |
> |---|---|
> | Tax reform | Expenditure taxes |
> | Distortion of choice | Consumers' surplus |
> | Minimum burden | Producers' surplus |
> | Excess burden | Deadweight loss |
> | Income tax | Head, poll or lump-sum tax |
> | Opportunity cost of leisure | Benefit approach |
> | Disincentives | Ability-to-pay approach |
> | Substitution effect | Equal sacrifice |
> | Income effect | Proportional |
> | Incentives | Progressive |
> | Supply side | Regressive |

Reading list

Boden, A., 'Taxation and Welfare = Revision Exercise, *Journal of the Economics Association*, Spring, 1992.

Healey, N., and Levačić Chapter 5 in *Supply Side Economics*, 2nd edn, Heinemann Educational, 1992.

Smith, D., Chapter 4 in *Mrs Thatcher's Economics: Her Legacy*, 2nd edn, Heinemann Educational, 1992.

Essay topics

1. 'There are two microeconomic criteria by which to assess a tax – efficiency and equity.' With reference to these criteria, examine the effects of: (i) a reduction of the higher income tax rate, and (ii) an increase in the duty payable on cigarettes. (Joint Matriculation Board, A/S level, 1990)

2. What do you understand by the term 'standard of living' and how can it be measured? To what extent, if any, have recent changes in the government's taxation policies affected the standard of living in UK households? (Joint Matriculation Board, A/S level, 1992)

3. Distinguish between income and wealth. Discuss the possible economic effects of policies aimed at significantly reducing inequalities in income and wealth. (Associated Examining Board, 1991)

4. Under what circumstances might a government decide to increase taxes? What criteria are relevant when considering the relative merits of direct and indirect taxes? (University of London Examinations and Assessment Council, 1991)

5. 'The Conservative government's consistent aim has been to bring down the tax burden when it is prudent to do so, and in particular to reduce the basic rate of income tax. Progress has been considerable.' (Conservative Party Campaign Guide, April 1991). Discuss. (Oxford and Cambridge Schools Examination Board, 1992)

Data Response Question 7

Study the table which shows rates of income tax in three different financial years in the UK.

	1975/76		1979/80		1989/90	
	Band of taxable income	Rate %	Band of taxable income	Rate %	Band of taxable income	Rate %
Lower			1–750**	25		
Basic	1–4,500	35	751–10,000	30	1–20,700	25
Higher	4,501–5,000	40	10,001–12,000	40	Over 20,700	40
	5,001–6,000	45	12,001–15,000	45		
	6,001–7,000	50	15,001–20,000	50		
	7,001–8,000	55	20,001–25,000	55		
	8,001–10,000	60	Over 25,000	60		
	10,001–12,000	65				
	12,001–15,000	70				
	15,001–20,000	75				
	Over 20,000	83*				

* Top rate lowered from 83% in 1978/79.
** Lowest band of taxable income removed in 1980/81.
Source: An Economic Profile of Britain, Lloyds Bank plc, 1990.

1. Describe the main changes in income tax over the period shown in the table.
2. Would you consider the income tax structure to be more or less progressive in 1979/80 than in 1989/90? Explain your answer.
3. Assume that in 1989/90 every tax payer had a tax free allowance of £3000. For a person with a gross income of £30 000, what was: (i) the average rate of tax; (ii) the marginal rate of tax?
4. Compare the tax structure existing in 1979/80 with that in 1989/90 in terms of: (i) incentives to work; (ii) the distribution of income; (iii) obtaining the highest level of tax revenue.

(University of London Examinations and Assessment Council 1993)

Chapter Eight
Poverty and redistribution

'Fair play with the cake, you know' said the Lion.   Lewis Carroll

Definitions of poverty

The terms 'poverty' and 'poor' are value-laden and there is no agreement about their meaning ... poverty refers in a general way to those at the bottom end of the income distribution. (Sixth Report of the Social Security Advisory Committee, 1988)

Two alternative definitions may be offered. The first sees **poverty** as a condition of acute deprivation where people do not even have enough to eat. This is absolute poverty or **starvation poverty**. The alternative defines poverty as a condition of **relative deprivation**: in this state, though people may have enough to eat, their standard of living is so far below the average that they cannot obtain what may generally be regarded as necessities of life, like television sets and disposable nappies. They are 'excluded from the conditions of life which ordinarily define membership of society'.

Today poverty is defined in this second way. Indeed the idea of absolute poverty is a difficult one to sustain. 'The necessities of life are not fixed.' 'People do not live by bread alone; sometimes they are prepared to forgo bread for more pressing social needs' (P. Townsend). These ideas give us the idea of **subsistence poverty** which is related to the general standard of living. Those in subsistence poverty have incomes below the level regarded as necessary for membership of society. Until the 1980s this was clearly recognized by governments which uprated benefits in line with earnings. In the eighties benefits have risen in line with price inflation which is usually below wage inflation.

The level of supplementary benefit, now **income support**, was an objective measure of the border between adequate subsistence and poverty. However, particularly since the separation of benefits from earnings, and the replacement of single payments by loans from the cash-limited Social Fund, many people consider that the state social security system no longer keeps everyone on benefits out of subsistence poverty. The extract in the box entitled 'Church, state and poverty' illustrates the issue.

Church, state and poverty

Living Faith in the City, the Church of England's latest analysis of Britain's social problems, is certain to irritate members of the UK government. It is strongly critical of recent tax and social security reforms, which it says have greatly increased the gap between rich and poor. Many underprivileged people, it suggests, face a bleaker future today than they did in the mid-1980s.

The bulk of the population has undoubtedly enjoyed rapidly rising living standards in the past decade. But this general prosperity has been accompanied by acute social disorders: rising inner city crime, more begging on the streets, an increase in one-parent families, and widespread homelessness.

The study is deeply critical of the concept of poverty advanced by Mr John Moore, the former Social Services Secretary. Mr Moore pointed out that 50 per cent of those on income support have a telephone and almost all have a television. To talk of poverty in modern Britain, he suggested, was a "dangerous" misuse of language. The church's response is that poverty is a "relative as well as an absolute concept". It exists "even in a relatively rich western society if people are denied access to what is generally regarded as a reasonable standard and quality of life in that society." It is about powerlessness, exclusion and loss of dignity, as well as shortage of money.

The authors of *Living Faith in the City* are therefore concerned by the sharp rise in inequality during the 1980s. Between April 1979 and April 1989, the real weekly earnings of the lowest paid decile rose 5.7 per cent; the top decile enjoyed an increase of 36.6 per cent. Over the same period, the income tax liabilities of the lowest decile fell by 1.6 per cent; those of the top decile fell by 48.5 per cent. "In our judgment", says the report, "the inequalities are too great and are excluding more and more from participating in our society."

Source: *Financial Times*, 31 Jan. 1990

Causes of poverty

People's incomes are determined by the **resources** (factors) they own, and by the prices the market puts on the services of those resources. Though some own **land** and **capital assets,** for most people their main wealth is their own labour power (**human capital**) and their income is labour income (wages). Poverty is caused by a lack of real resources, principally human capital. Either lack of skills and training make available only low-paid employment; or old age, extreme youth, sickness and disability, or having young children to care for make employment impossible; or there may be no jobs. The causes of poverty are therefore linked to circumstances which put people with no other resources at a disadvantage in the labour market. Old age, large family size, being single and female, being a one-parent family, being sick or disabled or unemployed, or being a member of a disadvantaged ethnic minority group, are all associated with poverty.

Income shares

Table 2 from *Social Trends* shows **income distribution** in Britain in 1977 and 1988 before and after the effects of government intervention. As we are concerned with relative incomes, shares in the total rather than absolute amounts are given. For each of the two years the first row gives the shares of original income and the second row gives final income shares after cash benefits and taxes. At the end of the 1980s the share of income before state intervention going to the poorest quintile (fifth) of the population, and their share after benefits and taxes, were lower than in 1977. In 1977 the poorest 20 per cent had 4 per cent of original income and 9 per cent of income after benefits and taxes; in 1988 they had 2 per cent and 7 per cent respectively.

Table 2 Income distribution in the UK, 1977, 1988

Income shares, percent

	Quintile groups of households (ranked by equivalized disposable income)				
	Bottom fifth	*Next fifth*	*Middle fifth*	*Next fifth*	*Top fifth*
1977					
Equivalized original income*	4	10	18	26	43
Equivalized income after cash benefits received and taxes paid	9	14	17	23	37
1988					
Equivalized original income	2	7	16	25	50
Equivalized income after cash benefits received and taxes paid	7	11	16	22	44

* Original income is income from employment, occupational persons and investments. 'Equivalized' means adjusted for household size and composition.
Taxes paid include income tax, NICs, domestic rates and estimated indirect taxes (VAT and excise duties)
Source: *CSO Social Trends*, 1992

Policy options

Most people would agree that equity demands that there should be some **redistribution** of income to relieve poverty, though there are differences of view on which of the poor should be helped and how much help they should get. However, policies to mitigate poverty may give rise to distortions which reduce total welfare (inefficiency). A fairer distribution of the cake *might* lead to a reduction in its size.

There are two principal ways of relieving poverty: **fiscal methods** (taxes and transfers) and **market intervention** (in both product and factor markets). Fiscal methods mean that taxes must be raised for redistribution and these are distortionary (see Chapter 7). Additionally on the transfers side, benefit payments also cause inefficiences – for example the disincentive effects of the poverty trap. Market methods change prices:

* Rent controls to help the poor get affordable housing may keep rents below the equilibrium.
* Minimum wage legislation may keep some wage rates above equilibrium.
* Minimum prices for agricultural products (to raise farm incomes) may prevent equilibrium.

However, Figure 4 in Chapter 2 shows that efficiency (maximum welfare) requires that price is where the supply (marginal social benefit) and demand (marginal social cost) curves intersect; thus market interventions can reduce *total* welfare. In this chapter we illustrate the problem by focusing on one of the most important market intervention policies, **minimum wages**. Then we look at another instance of government action where legislation does *not* reduce efficiency: banning discrimination in the labour market can improve both equity and efficiency simultaneously.

Minimum wages: equity and efficiency in conflict

A firm aiming to maximize profits will employ a worker if the revenue gained from selling what he or she produces is greater than the wage which must be paid. The revenue a firm gets from an additional worker's output is the **marginal revenue product** (MRP). The MRP curve slopes down from left to right as in Figure 19, on p.92, because it is derived from the marginal physical product of labour (MPP_L). This declines as additional workers are employed because, in the short run, diminishing returns set in.

If the marginal revenue product and the wage are plotted on the same diagram (*y* axis, Figure 19) we can see how the MRP schedule becomes

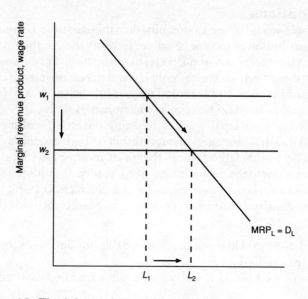

Figure 19 The labour demand schedule

the labour demand schedule. A profit-maximizing firm will employ all workers whose MRP is greater than the wage they must be paid; if the wage is W_1 employment will be at L_1. Up to L_1 each worker adds more to revenue than they cost (MRP > W); beyond L_1 they would cost more than the revenue earned from what they produce (MRP < W). However, if the wage fell to L_2 it would become profitable to employ the marginal workers between L_1 and L_2. Thus the MRP curve shows what quantity of labour will be employed at each wage – it is the demand curve for labour.

The wage which a firm faces is determined in the **labour market** for workers with the skills they require. The equilibrium wage for an occupation is determined by demand and supply. The demand curve is the sum of firms' demand curves and the supply curve is the sum of individual supply curves, with these representing the marginal opportunity cost of labour (MC_L). MC_L to an occupation is the wage forgone elsewhere; MC_L to the whole economy is the marginal cost (disutility) of work to the worker.

The effect of minimum wage legislation is shown in Figure 20. If a minimum wage has to be paid which is above the equilibrium, employment falls. Only employees between 0 and L_0 produce revenue greater than the minimum wage. Between L_0 and L_e the returns from selling what each worker produces would be below the wage which must be paid. And so jobs are lost, employment is at L_0.

This situation is inefficient because, between L_0 and L_e, the value of output each additional worker would produce (MRP_L) is greater than the cost (MC_L). For the marginal worker at L_0 the difference is ac. The **deadweight loss** of welfare is the shaded area ace. Both workers and employers lose: if the market determined the wage there would be more jobs; all workers would receive a wage greater than the marginal cost to them of working; and the employer would sell output for more than the wage paid.

Most economists, irrespective of their political views, do not favour minimum wages. They argue that while they destroy jobs they do little to help family poverty because the majority of those who would gain are young people and second wage-earners who are not from poor households. Economists prefer fiscal means to alleviate poverty. The view of those who argue that we should seek a high-wage/high-skills economy is not rejected, but it puts the cart before the horse to say that high wages lead to high skills. Skills training and higher productivity must come first, otherwise higher wages destroy jobs. The box labelled 'Minimum wages: a cautionary tale of north and south' contains all the arguments which most economists today would subscribe to.

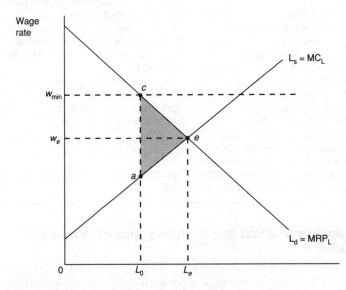

Figure 20 The efects of minimum wage legislation on employment

Minimum wages: a cautionary tale of north and south

Richard Layard

Today, most northern European countries support "upward harmonisation" of wages in the rest of Europe. If this happens, the industrial blossoming of the European south will be blighted.

Yet this is the implication of the European Community's Social Chapter. In this context, Britain is part of the south.

The situation is made worse by the threat of an EC directive on minimum wages. Worse still, the British Labour Party has now been converted to a statutory minimum wage.

A change of this kind could have a devastating effect on the employment of less-skilled people. It is absurd to assert that competitiveness matters (as all do) and then to pretend that only the productivity element in competitiveness matters, and not the element of labour costs. . . .

There are of course countries where pay is much more equal than in Britain and yet unemployment is lower. Sweden is the clearest example. But there massive resources have been devoted to raising the skill levels of the less able, and further major efforts are made to help the unemployed. . . .

Of course, there are those who say that unemployment does not matter. If people cannot be employed at a reasonable wage, they say, it is better that they be unemployed, living on benefit. This argument is misleading on at least four grounds.

First, it involves economic waste. Second it overlooks the effect on a person's self-respect of a prolonged job search while being dependent on benefits. Third, it assumes that the same people remain on low wages indefinitely, while in fact there is substantial mobility.

Fourth, and most serious, it greatly exaggerates the relation between poverty and low pay. This is because a person's poverty depends on the earnings of all family members relative to the family's size. Thus, it does not necessarily follow that the families of the low paid are poor. Neither is the reverse true. Only one in five of the working poor are low-paid, and vice versa.

It follows that reducing low pay will have quite small effects on the overall distribution of income. Some poor people will gain, but some will lose through increased unemployment.

Poverty has to be attacked by fiscal measures and not by a minimum wage, which will leave it largely untouched. . . .

Any warm-hearted person is bound to favour minimum wages until he thinks of all their effects. There is yet time to think these through.

Professor Layard is with the London School of Economics

Source: *Financial Times*, 22 Nov. 1989

Anti-discrimination laws: equity and efficiency coincide

The arguments over minimum wages illustrate the conflict between equity and efficiency. However, though such conflict is common, there are circumstances where improving equity also brings greater efficiency. For example, legislation to ban **discrimination** in the labour market on the grounds of race or sex is fair and efficient.

At its most extreme, discrimination results in a **dual labour market** with black people or women being excluded from the main labour market. In the segregated market where they are forced to work their marginal product is lower than it would be in the main labour market. If discrimination were outlawed people would move from jobs where they were less productive to jobs where they were more productive. Total output and total welfare would rise; in particular, as they could earn more, the welfare of those previously discriminated against would increase. There are gains in both equity and efficiency.

With discrimination, wages and employment in each labour market is at W_1L_1 in Figure 21. In the main market, from which disadvantaged workers are excluded, wages and productivity (denoted by MRP) are higher than in the segregated market. When discrimination is made illegal (and there is access to skills training) workers move from lower-wage/lower-productivity employment to higher-wage/higher-productivity jobs. Employment falls in the previously segregated market and rises in the main labour market (to L_2 in each case); wages rise in the segregated market and fall in the main market (to W_2 in each case). Overall there is a welfare gain because the rise in the value of output in the main market (shaded area) is greater than the fall in the value of output in the segregated market (shaded area).

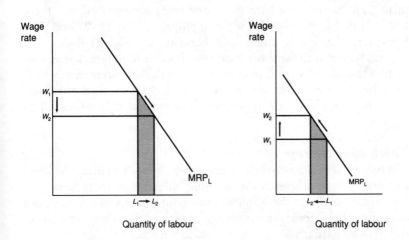

(a) Main labour market   (b) Segregated labour market

Figure 21 The consequences of anti-discrimination measures

Fiscal redistribution: taxes and transfers

It is fair to tax those with jobs and incomes, and to make transfers to those without either, or with low incomes and large families or other special needs. But raising taxes and paying benefits both involve inefficiencies. The disincentive effects of taxation were discussed in Chapter 7. Here we turn to the benefits side.

In the UK **social security** transfers are either **contributory benefits** (retirement pensions, sickness and unemployment benefits) obtained as of right by those who have made National Insurance contributions, or **means-tested** (now called 'income-related' or 'targeted') **non-contributory** benefits which people have to prove a need for (income support, housing benefit, family credit). Child benefit and attendance allowances are universal non-contributory benefits and fall into neither category.

Though there are many problems affecting the whole of the social security system, it is particularly the means-tested benefits which give rise to important efficiency issues. Two disincentives in particular have been identified: the 'poverty trap' which affects the working poor, and the 'unemployment trap' which affects the unemployed.

The **unemployment trap** refers to the effect of the tax and benefits system making income when out of work little different from income when in work, so that there is no great financial incentive for the unemployed to seek work. There has never been an unemployment trap for the long-term (over one year) unemployed, but there was a trap for the short-term unemployed in the 1960s and 70s. However, changes to taxes and benefits in 1982 abolished the unemployment trap for short-term as well as for long-term unemployment. Only about 3 per cent of families (unskilled parent, many children) have income when out-of-work approaching the level of income when in work. The unemployment trap may now be regarded as a myth.

The poverty trap

The **poverty trap** is no myth. It affects low-paid workers in employment and presents the efficiency versus equity dilemma in acute form. It is fair to give benefits to the families of low-paid workers to help them out of poverty, but if these are withdrawn as income rises there is no incentive to work harder and earn more, which is inefficient.

The means-tested transfers available to help low-paid workers support their families are Family Credit and Housing Benefit (and council tax benefit). If a claimant works longer hours or gets a better paid job, the tax and benefit systems interact to make the rewards for doing so

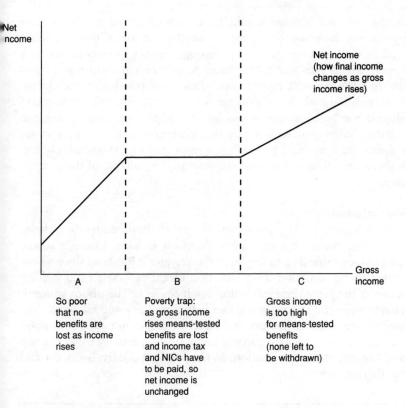

Net income (how final income changes as gross income rises)

A	B	C
So poor that no benefits are lost as income rises	Poverty trap: as gross income rises means-tested benefits are lost and income tax and NICs have to be paid, so net income is unchanged	Gross income is too high for means-tested benefits (none left to be withdrawn)

Figure 22 The poverty trap

very small, or (up to 1988) even negative. As income rises direct tax payments, which start at very low incomes, increase and benefits are withdrawn; net income changes very little. Figure 22 is a stylized version of the poverty trap.

In the UK in the 1990s the implicit 'rate of tax' in the area of the poverty trap is about 90 per cent. A £1 rise in gross income leads to a tax increase plus benefit withdrawal of about 90p, and a rise in net income of about 10p. This is an improvement on the situation before 1988 when the 1986 Social Security Act was implemented, when a £1 rise in gross earnings could lead to a fall in net income of more than £1.

The poverty trap is a fairly intractable problem. A Conservative government, much concerned with incentives and efficiency, managed to improve it a little, but the trap still exists. To make a greater difference between income at the bottom of the trap and income at the top, net income would have to be reduced at the bottom by cutting benefits, or increased at the top by a more gradual withdrawal of benefits or by raising the tax threshold so that benefit withdrawal and tax payment do not coincide. Cutting benefits would make the working poor even poorer and penalize their children. More gradual withdrawal of benefits would make many more workers eligible for benefits and would be very expensive. And raising the tax threshold would mainly help the non-poor (as all taxpayers would benefit) and it would deprive the government of a great deal of revenue. It seems that there are no easy answers to the problem of the poverty trap.

Conclusions

It is easy to say 'Fair play with the cake', but frequently policies which cut the cake more fairly diminish its size. Conflict is not always inevitable. For example, in this chapter it has been shown how making labour market discrimination illegal can raise total welfare while at the same time increasing the incomes of the disadvantaged. However, in the 1980s the conflict between equity and efficiency was particularly evident: the tax and benefit changes intended as supply-side incentives increased income inequalities, particularly at the top and bottom of the distribution, so the poor got relatively poorer and the rich got richer.

KEY WORDS

Poverty	Marginal revenue product
Starvation poverty	Labour market
Relative deprivation	Deadweight loss
Subsistence poverty	Discrimination
Income support	Dual labour market
Resources	Social security
Land	Contributory benefits
Capital assets	Means-tested
Human capital	Income-related
Income distribution	Targeted
Redistribution	Non-contributory benefits
Fiscal methods	Unemployment trap
Market intervention	Poverty trap
Minimum wages	

Reading list

Borooah, V. K. 'Poverty', *Economic Review*, Nov. 1991.

Johnson, P., 'Measuring poverty', *Economic Review*, Nov. 1990.

Marshall, P., 'Poverty and inequality', *Journal of the Economics Association*, summer, 1992.

Paisley, R., and Quillfeldt, J., Exercise 25 in *Economics Investigated*, vol. 2, Collins Educational, 1992.

Whynes, D., Chapter 3 in *Welfare State Economics*, Heinemann Educational, 1992.

Essay topics

1. Outline briefly the causes of differences in the wage rates paid to workers of different age, sex, race and skill in different industries and occupations. Discuss the possible effects of the introduction of a national minimum wage in the UK. (Joint Matriculation Board, 1992)
2. What is meant by stating that poverty is a relative concept? Assess the extent to which central and local government policies can relieve poverty in the UK. (Joint Matriculation Board, A/S level, 1992)
3. How does economic theory explain why some groups of workers are paid more than others? Discuss whether this theory explains why women are often paid less than men. (Associated Examining Board, 1991)
4. 'The UK's taxation and welfare benefits systems have trapped the low-waged in relative poverty and the unwaged in unemployment.' Explain the causes of this situation. Explain how problems created by this situation might be reduced. (Associated Examining Board, 1991)

Data Response Question 8

Poverty in Britain

This task is based on a question set by the Oxford and Cambridge Schools Examination Board in 1990. Read the two articles and answer the following questions.

1. Define (i) official poverty line, (ii) Income Support, (iii) poverty trap, (iv) net income, and (v) marginal tax rate.
2. What light do the above extracts throw on the causes of poverty in Britain? Can these arguments over the extent of poverty be reconciled?

Poverty in Britain has increased sharply since 1979, and a growing proportion are long-term poor. By 1985 (the latest available figures), 9.4 million people, including 2.25 million children, were living at or below the official poverty line. This is 17% of the population – an increase of 55% since 1979.

In 1985, over 15 million people were living in poverty or on its margins (up to 40% above the Supplementary Benefit [now Income Support] scale). This is 28% of the population.

In 1989, half a million families are caught in the poverty trap. For a couple with two children, if gross weekly earnings rise from £30.40 (when Housing Benefit starts to fall) to £165.90 (when Family Credit runs out), net income only rises from £126.20 to £143.70. An earnings rise of £135.50 increases net income by only £17.50. The effect of means-tested benefits is equivalent to a marginal tax rate of 87% over the whole income range.

(Source: Fabian Society, 1989)

Are the poor 'getting poorer'? No, they are not. It is clear that people at all income levels now have substantially more money to spend in real terms than they did in the 1970s. In fact by almost every material measure it is possible to contrive – health, longevity, real income, ownership of consumer durables, number and length of holidays, money spent on entertainment, numbers in further education – not only are those with lower incomes not getting poorer, they are substantially better off than they have ever been before. Strong economic growth, coupled with cuts in income tax, have helped raise living standards to record levels. For a family with two children in the bottom 10% of the earnings league, real take-home pay has risen by almost 14% since 1979. The real incomes of the poorest tenth of the whole population rose by 8.3% between 1981 and 1985 (the latest available figures). Total spending on benefits has now increased by 33% in real terms since 1978/9.

(Source: Conservative Research Department, 1989)

Index